GOOD HOUSEKEEPING
BOOK OF
CASSEROLES

Compiled by GOOD HOUSEKEEPING INSTITUTE

EBURY PRESS · LONDON

First published 1972 by
Ebury Press
Chestergate House, Vauxhall Bridge Road,
London SW1V 1HF

© The National Magazine Co. Ltd. 1972

ISBN 0 85223 022 2

Photographs by Rex Barber, Anthony Blake, Frank Coppins,
John Street and Ken Swain. Front cover photo by Melvin Grey.
The photograph of Bengal Curry on page 102 is reproduced by
courtesy of the U.S. Rice Association.

Photoset by Typesetting Services Ltd, Glasgow, and
printed and bound in Italy by Interlitho, s.p.a., Milan.

GOOD HOUSEKEEPING
Book of Casseroles

A piping hot casserole straight from the oven – the ideal family meal for a cold winter's day. Equally, casseroled meals are the perfect solution for the working wife who likes to entertain. Subtle use of herbs and spices can turn the most economical cuts of meat into delicious meals with the minimum of effort. Casseroles have certainly come a long way from the days of 'just another name for stew' – and contained here are over 180 recipes for all occasions, each one double-tested in Good Housekeeping Institute's own kitchens. There are chapters covering meat, fish, and poultry casseroles for the family; classic French dishes for a formal dinner party; even chapters dealing with casseroled vegetables and fruit.

As an added bonus, a whole section on curries gives many traditional dishes, both mild and hot, as well as some of the more usual accompaniments which round off a curry meal.

All the recipes are in the usual, easy-to-follow style cooks have come to expect from Good Housekeeping Institute, and over 40 full colour photographs show clearly how to present the completed dish.

Contents

Foreword

Here for the first time is a collection of Good Housekeeping's favourite casserole and curry recipes. These have been gathered from all over the world and then tried and tested in the famous Good Housekeeping Institute kitchens. We've even surprised ourselves by the variety of dishes we've found, ranging from old-time standbys like traditional Lancashire Hotpot and Irish Stew to exotic sounding recipes for Pork with Sauerkraut and Juniper Berries, Couscous from Morocco, and Chicken Gumbo.

One of the delights of casserole cookery is the excellent choice of good-looking oven-to-table dishes. Choose the kind you like the look of best – copper, flameproof china, brightly coloured enamel, earthenware or ovenproof glass – the flavour of your stews will be just the same, as long as the casserole has a well-fitting lid. Remember, however, before you put the china, glass or earthenware variety onto a gas burner or hot plate to check that it is marked flameproof. The cooking times on the recipes have been given as a guide but most casseroles will come to no harm if they are left to cook longer at a lower temperature. But remember that flour-thickened sauces tend to separate with prolonged cooking so with these recipes it's better to leave the thickening until just before you serve – unless you're going to watch the time carefully.

If you own a home freezer, you'll find casseroles are among the most useful things to have in it and also one of the least troublesome to prepare. You can always make twice the recipe quantity and have one casserole to eat and one to freeze. See that the meat is cooked but not overcooked, to allow for reheating. Do not season too heavily, as seasonings tend to get stronger during freezer storage. Have enough liquid or sauce to immerse the meat completely. When the mixture is quite cold pour it into a rigid container or a foil-lined casserole (this is the most convenient) and freeze solid. Then slip the foil and the contents out of the casserole, over-wrap in polythene, label, and store. To reheat simply peel off the foil and put the frozen food into the original casserole. Allow $1\frac{1}{2}$–2 hours in the oven at 235°F (mark 3) or until it is bubbling hot.

If you have any queries about the recipes in this book write to us at Good Housekeeping Institute, Chestergate House, Vauxhall Bridge Road, London SW1V 1HF.

CAROL MACARTNEY
Principal

CHAPTER 1

Meat: Stews, Casseroles and Hotpots

To make a hearty meal that will please the whole family, you can use the most economical cuts of meat – best or scrag end of neck, shin of beef, spare ribs – and ring the changes with different flavourings and subtle seasoning. This chapter offers a selection of over thirty meat-based dishes – some of them simple, easy-to-cook family meals, others more elaborate for when you have company. Though we give the cooking temperature and time, in almost every case the casserole will taste equally delicious if you turn down the temperature and cook it for longer than stated – a useful thing to bear in mind, if your family's movements are more than a little uncertain!

Beef and Kidney Casserole

1 lb. stewing steak
½ lb. kidney
Plain flour
Salt and pepper
2 oz. lard or dripping
2 medium-sized onions, skinned and
    sliced

¼ lb. mushrooms, sliced
½ lb. potatoes, diced
¾ pint stock
A 5-oz. pkt. of frozen peas to garnish
    (optional)

OVEN TEMPERATURE: 350°F (mark 4)

Trim the steak and kidney, cut into even-sized cubes and coat with seasoned flour. Melt the fat, fry the sliced onions till tender, remove and place in a casserole. Fry the meat until brown and put this also into the casserole. Add the mushrooms and potatoes and pour the stock over. Cook in the oven for about 2 hours, add the peas (if used) and cook for a further 15–20 minutes. *Serves 4*

Hotpot of Beef Olives with Orange

¾ lb. rump steak
Fat for frying
2 carrots, peeled and diced
2 sticks of celery, chopped
¼ lb. peas
Stock
Cornflour or plain flour to thicken

FOR THE FILLING
2 oz. mushrooms, chopped
Grated rind of ½ orange
Salt and pepper
2–3 tomatoes, chopped
2 tbsps. breadcrumbs

OVEN TEMPERATURE: 350°F (mark 4)

Trim the meat and beat until thin, then cut into strips. Prepare the filling by mixing all the ingredients together, adding seasoning to taste. Spread the filling on the strips of meat, roll each up and tie with cotton. Fry lightly in the hot fat and place in an ovenproof dish. Add the diced carrots, celery, and peas, half-cover with stock and cook in the oven for about 1½ hours.

Remove the cottons, thicken the gravy with cornflour or flour, and serve with the beef olives. *Serves 3–4.*

Planked Braised Beef

A 3-lb. piece of top ribs beef, boned and trimmed

MARINADE:
1 medium onion, sliced
3 carrots, sliced
3 small cloves garlic, peeled and crushed
2 bay leaves
Rosemary

Parsley sprigs
Strip of orange peel
3 cloves
1 tbsp. wine vinegar
¼ pint red wine (Burgundy or Claret style)
Salt and freshly ground pepper
Cooking oil
3–4 level tsps. arrowroot

OVEN TEMPERATURE: 300°F (mark 2)

Choose a piece of beef about 2½ in. thick, trimmed free of surplus fat. Leave to marinade overnight in a covered casserole, using marinade ingredients. Next morning drain off the marinade. Dust beef with flour and seal surfaces in hot oil. Drain from the oil. Place in a casserole just large enough to take the meat and marinade, the latter to come half way up the meat. Cover and cook for about 3 hours until tender. Take meat from casserole, slice, and return to shape. Keep warm. Strain liquor and thicken with arrowroot.

To serve, pipe creamed potato round the edge of a thick hard board or plate. Protect the centre with foil and brown potatoes under the grill. Remove foil. Place meat in centre, coat with hot gravy. Sprinkle with parsley. Garnish with onions, carrots, and mushrooms. Serve extra gravy in a sauceboat. *Serves 6.*

Rich Beef and Tomato Casserole

1½ lb. chuck steak
1 level tbsp. dry mustard
2 level tbsps. flour
Oil for frying
1 level tsp. dried garlic chips
1 small onion, skinned and finely chopped
2 caps canned pimiento (sweet red peppers)

2 tbsps. chopped celery leaves
1 tbsp. chopped parsley
¼ pint tomato chutney
¾ pint water
2 level tbsps. demerara sugar
Pinch of cayenne pepper
¼ lb. button mushrooms
Creamy mashed potato
Celery leaves for garnish

OVEN TEMPERATURE: 300°F (mark 2)

Planked Braised Beef

Trim excess fat from steak, cut into largish pieces. Toss in a mixture of mustard and flour. In a frying-pan, put just enough oil to cover the base of the pan. Fry meat until well coloured. Meanwhile in a saucepan mix together the remainder of the ingredients, except the mushrooms and potato, and boil for 10 minutes. Put meat in a cas-serole, pour the boiled ingredients over. Cover tightly and cook in the oven for about 2½ hours until meat is fork tender.

Stir in the whole sautéd mushrooms. Use creamed potato to form a collar round the edge. Brown quickly under a hot grill. Garnish with celery leaves. *Serves 4.*

Glazed Topside

4 slices topside of beef (about 1¼ lb.)
2 tbsps. cooking oil
A 14-oz. can tomatoes
1 level tbsp. flour

1 tbsp. chutney
Onion-salt and pepper
Chopped parsley
1 hard-boiled egg, chopped (optional)

OVEN TEMPERATURE: 325°F (mark 3)

Bat out the slices of beef to about ⅛–¼ in. thickness. Cut each in half. Coat the base of a shallow flameproof casserole with the oil. When hot, quickly and lightly brown the beef a few pieces at a time. Drain and keep beef on one side. Add the tomatoes and their juice to pan juices, dredge with the flour, add chutney, stir, and bring to the boil. Season to taste with onion-salt and pepper. Arrange the beef slices overlapping one another over the tomato mixture. Bring to the boil. Cover tightly. Place in the centre of the oven for about 1 hour or until the beef is fork tender. Keep slices of beef to one side. Spoon off any excess fat from the juices. Check seasoning.

Bring to the boil on top of the cooker, stirring. Return the beef slices to the cas-serole the opposite way up so that the moist side is uppermost. Reheat, and garnish with chopped parsley and hard-boiled egg. *Serves 3–4.*

Marinated Steak Pot

2 lb. chuck steak
2 tbsps. garlic vinegar
2 oz. dripping
1½ oz. flour
¼ lb. button mushrooms, stalked
¼ lb. streaky bacon, rinded and diced

¼ lb. button onions, skinned
1 pint beef stock
Bay leaf
1 tbsp. concentrated tomato paste
Bouquet garni
Chopped parsley

OVEN TEMPERATURE: 325°F (mark 3)

Lamb Julienne (*see page* 26), Rich Beef and Tomato Casserole (*see page* 10) and Pork Chops with Orange (*see page* 18)

Cut the meat into neat pieces, place in a polythene bag with the vinegar. Toss meat inside bag and put bag in a deep bowl; leave overnight to marinate.

Melt dripping in a frying pan. Drain meat and dry on absorbent paper (reserve juices), toss in the flour, and fry until sealed and brown. Remove meat. To the pan, add the onions, mushrooms, and bacon and fry for 5 minutes. Place with the meat and juices in a tightly-lidded casserole. Pour the stock into the frying pan, stir to loosen sediment, add the bay leaf, tomato paste, and bouquet garni. Bring to the boil and pour over the meat. Cover tightly and cook in the oven for about 1½ hours.

Discard bay leaf and bouquet garni. Serve sprinkled generously with chopped parsley. *Serves 6.*

Beef Hotpot

Beef Hotpot

1 lb. shin of beef
1½ oz. lard
¼ lb. carrots, scraped and sliced
¼ lb. button mushrooms, stalked
Salt and pepper

¼ lb. onions, skinned and sliced
½ oz. flour
¼ pint water
1 lb. old potatoes, peeled and sliced
Chopped parsley

OVEN TEMPERATURE: 350°F (mark 4)

Cut trimmed beef into 2-in. strips. Heat the lard in a frying-pan, add meat and fry until evenly browned. Put drained meat into a 4-pint casserole with carrots, mushroom caps, and chopped stalks. Season. Fry the onion in the remaining fat in the pan until golden brown; add to casserole. Stir the flour into the fat in the pan and slowly pour in the water. Bring to the boil and simmer for a few minutes. Arrange potatoes in overlapping rings on top of the other ingredients to cover the surface completely. Strain the gravy over the potatoes, cover, and cook for about 2 hours.

15 minutes before the end, remove the lid and raise temperature to 400°F (mark 6) to brown the potatoes. *Serves 4.*

Swiss Steak

1 tbsp. oil
2 large onions, skinned and sliced
1½ lb. chuck or blade-bone steak
Salt and pepper

1 oz. flour
8 tomatoes, skinned
An 8-oz. can tomato juice
Parsley for garnish

OVEN TEMPERATURE: 350°F (mark 4)

Heat the oil in a frying-pan and sauté the onions until transparent. (If a flameproof casserole is available this can be used throughout the cooking.) Trim the steak and cut into 8 portions. Dredge with seasoned flour and brown in the oil. Add the tomatoes and tomato juice. Stir well to loosen the drippings from pan. Turn into a casserole, cover, and cook in the oven for 1½–2 hours.

Garnish with parsley. *Serves 4.*

Brisket Pot-Roast

A 2¾-lb. piece of brisket, rolled
Seasoned flour
1 oz. dripping or lard
2 tbsps. red wine
2 tbsps. stock
Bay leaf

4 peppercorns
4 cloves
1 lb. carrots, skinned and sliced
1 lb. small onions, peeled
2 oz. butter
Salt and pepper

OVEN TEMPERATURE: 300°F (mark 2)

Coat the brisket lightly in seasoned flour. Heat the dripping in a pan. Add the meat and fry, turning to ensure even browning. Transfer to a large piece of greased foil on a baking sheet, turn up foil at edges then pour the wine and stock over the meat. Add the bay leaf, peppercorns, and cloves and bring edges together, folding over to seal tightly. Cook for about 2½ hours.

In separate packages, cook sliced carrots and small onions (with 1 oz. butter each and seasoning) alongside the meat for the last hour. *Serves 4.*

Steak Hotpot, Pork Hotpot (*see page* 20) and Chicken Hotpot (*see page* 44)

Steak Hotpot

1 lb. stewing steak
2 oz. fat
1 onion, skinned and diced
1 stick of celery, diced

½ lb. carrots, peeled and sliced
1 orange, grated
Salt and pepper

OVEN TEMPERATURE: 350°F (mark 4)

Cut the steak into ¾-in. cubes and fry in the hot fat until brown on every side. Transfer the meat to a casserole. Sauté the diced onion and celery until golden brown. Put onion, celery, and carrots in the casserole, with the orange rind and the juice from half the orange. Add salt and pepper and half-cover with water. Cut the remaining half-orange into slices, halve these, arrange round the edge of the hotpot, and cook in oven for 2 hours. *Serves 4.*

Braised Beef with Soured Cream and Mushrooms

$3\frac{1}{2}$ lb. thick flank beef
A 14-oz. can plum tomatoes
2 beef stock cubes
$\frac{1}{2}$ lb. onions, skinned and quartered
$\frac{1}{2}$ lb. carrots, peeled and halved

1 lb. button mushrooms
2 oz. butter
1 or 2 cartons (5-fl. oz. each) soured cream
Chopped parsley for garnish

OVEN TEMPERATURE: 325°F (mark 3)

Trim the flank free of fat and cut the lean into thin strips. Into a wide flameproof casserole (4-pint) – the contents should be in a shallow layer – pour the contents of the can of tomatoes.

Crumble in the stock cubes. Arrange meat in the centre with carrot, onion, and mushroom stalks at the side. Cover tightly, preferably with foil and a lid. Cook in the oven for 2 hours. Remove lid and gently turn meat in the juice. Cover, reduce heat to 300°F (mark 2) and cook a further hour until tender.

Slice mushrooms thickly. Sauté in butter. Discard onion, carrot, and mushroom stalks. On top of the cooker add mushrooms and stir in contents from 1 carton of soured cream. Reheat without boiling. Adjust seasoning; if wished stir in more soured cream and garnish with chopped parsley. *Serves 6.*

Pork Ribs with Spiced Sauce

2 lb. spare ribs – English cut
1 tbsp. oil
1 oz. butter
$\frac{1}{2}$ lb. onions, skinned and finely chopped
1 level tbsp. flour
$\frac{1}{2}$ level tsp. ground ginger

$\frac{1}{2}$ pint chicken stock
2 tbsps. white wine vinegar
An 8-oz. can cranberry sauce
$\frac{1}{4}$ level tsp. dried rosemary
Salt and freshly ground black pepper
Chopped parsley for garnish

OVEN TEMPERATURE: 325°F (mark 3)

Trim the spare ribs of excess fat. Heat the oil in a large frying-pan, add the butter and on the point of browning add the meat. Fry briskly and brown on both sides. Transfer to a casserole. Add the onions to the pan and sauté until tender, stir in the flour and ginger, and cook for 1 minute. Pour over the stock, vinegar, cranberry sauce, rosemary, salt, and pepper. Bring to the boil, stirring. Pour over the meat. Cover casserole and cook for 1½ hours.

Remove meat from casserole. Lift off fat by laying sheets of absorbent paper over the juices. Reduce juices by one-third. Return meat and reheat. Sprinkle with fresh parsley. *Serves 4.*

Pork and Prune Hotpot

¼ lb. prunes
Juice and rind of 1 lemon
1 lb. pork

1 oz. plain flour
Salt and pepper
½ oz. dripping

OVEN TEMPERATURE: 350°F (mark 4)

Cover the prunes with cold water, leave to soak for a few hours, then stew them with the rind of the lemon until tender. Strain off the juice and keep it. Remove the stones from the prunes.

Wipe the pork, cut it into neat pieces and pass these through the seasoned flour. Melt the dripping in a frying-pan and fry the

pork until brown. Place the pork and prunes in alternate layers in a casserole. Make some brown gravy with the remaining fat, flour, and about ½ pint of the prune juice and pour this over the pork. Add the lemon juice, cover the casserole tightly, and stew in the oven for about 1 hour. Serve in the casserole. *Serves 4.*

Pork Chops with Orange

4 large pork chump chops
2 level tbsps. seasoned flour
Oil for frying
2 large thin-skinned oranges
4 level tbsps. soft light brown sugar
1 level tbsp. cornflour

¼ pint dry white wine
½ pint orange juice
1 medium onion, skinned and sliced
Watercress or parsley sprigs for
  garnish

OVEN TEMPERATURE: 350°F (mark 4)

Trim chops, removing the rind. Coat in seasoned flour. Heat just enough oil in a large frying-pan to cover the base of the pan. Fry chops quickly on either side until well browned (two at a time if the pan is on the small side). Drain and place in a shallow casserole large enough to take a single layer. Remove rind and all traces of white pith from the oranges. Slice, discard pips, and

cut each slice in half. Place on a plate and sprinkle with 2 tbsps. sugar. Blend cornflour with a little wine, orange juice, and sugar. Bring to the boil, stirring. Pour over the chops. Arrange sliced onion over chops. Cover tightly and cook in the oven for 1¼–1½ hours.

Remove lid; arrange orange slices over onion. Continue to cook for a further 15–

20 minutes; baste occasionally. To serve, if wished reduce liquor by boiling, adjust seasoning and garnish with watercress or parsley sprigs. *Serves 4.*

Porkie Pot

1 lb. belly pork
1 tbsp. oil
6 oz. onion, skinned and chopped
1 lb. lamb's liver, diced
1 level tbsp. flour
¼ pint beef stock

A 14-oz. can tomato juice
1 clove of garlic, peeled and crushed
½ level tsp. dried basil or thyme
Bay leaf
1 tbsp. Worcestershire sauce
Chopped parsley for garnish

OVEN TEMPERATURE: 325°F (mark 3)

Rind and remove any bone from the pork; cut into 1-in. squares. Heat the oil in a flameproof casserole, add the pork and fry briefly until well browned. Remove pork, add onion and fry until tender. Add liver and flour, stir well, and return pork to casserole. Add beef stock, tomato juice, garlic, and other seasonings and bring to the boil, stirring. Transfer to the oven, cover, and cook for about 1½ hours.

Skim off fat, adjust seasoning and sprinkle with chopped parsley. *Serves 4.*

Paupiettes of Pork

2 6-oz. pork escalopes
2 oz. butter
2 oz. lean streaky bacon, rinded and diced
4 oz. onion, skinned and chopped
2 oz. fresh white breadcrumbs
4 oz. pork sausage meat
¼ level tsp. dried thyme

Salt and freshly ground black pepper
1 level tbsp. flour
1 tbsp. oil
3 tbsps. dry white wine
¼ level tsp. paprika
½ pint chicken stock
1 tbsp. cream

OVEN TEMPERATURE: 400°F (mark 6)

Beat escalopes between wetted greaseproof paper until fairly thin. Melt 1 oz. butter in a small pan, add the bacon and quarter of onion, sauté until soft. Cool. Combine with breadcrumbs, sausage meat, and thyme. Season and spread over meat. Roll up and tie with string. Toss rolls in flour. Heat oil in a small pan. Add 1 oz. butter. When beginning to colour, fry pork until evenly browned. Transfer to a small casserole. Reheat pan juices. Add 3 oz. onion, sauté until transparent. Stir in excess flour, wine, pinch of thyme, paprika, stock and cream. Bring to the boil, pour over the meat.

Cook in coolest part of oven for about 1¼ hours. Skim off excess fat using absorbent paper. Remove string. *Serves 2*

Pork Hotpot

4 loin pork chops
½ lb. cooking apples, cored and sliced
1 onion, sliced
2 oz. fat

3 tomatoes, peeled
1 lb. potatoes, peeled and diced
Salt and pepper

OVEN TEMPERATURE: 350°F (mark 4)

Bone and roll the chops. Fry the apples and onion in the fat until golden brown. Place the chops in a dish, cover with the apple and vegetables, add seasoning and half-cover the meat and vegetables with water. Cover the dish and cook in the oven for 1½ hours. *Serves 4.*

Schweinefleisch Rippchen auf Kraut

A traditional German dish of pork baked on sauerkraut with juniper berries.

A 3-lb. piece loin pork, salted
A 1-lb. 9-oz. can of sauerkraut, drained
1 oz. dripping
1 large onion, skinned and sliced

Bay leaf
Few juniper berries
Few caraway seeds
½ pint stock or water
Pinch of sugar

OVEN TEMPERATURE: 325°F (mark 3)

Pork Chops Oriental

Remove skin from pork, trim down the fat, and chine. Place sauerkraut in an oven-proof dish which will take meat. Melt dripping, sauté onion for a few minutes. Add to sauerkraut with bay leaf, berries, caraway seeds, stock, and sugar. Put meat on top, fat side uppermost; pour stock over. Cover and cook in the oven for about 1¾ hours.

Serve with boiled potatoes or potato dumplings. *Serves 4.*

Unsalted pork can be used if the butcher is not willing to salt it for you.

Pork Chops Oriental

1 tbsp. soy sauce
2 tbsps. sherry
1 level tbsp. light, soft brown sugar
1 clove garlic, peeled and crushed
2 pork chops (approx. 6 oz. each)
Oil
1 oz. butter

6 oz. onion, peeled and sliced
4 carrots, pared
1 level tbsp. flour
½ pint water
1 chicken stock cube
Chopped parsley and capers for garnish

OVEN TEMPERATURE: 325°F (mark 3)

In a cup, blend together the soy sauce, sherry, and sugar. Add crushed garlic. Trim the chops, pour the sherry mixture over and leave for 1 hour. Drain the chops, retaining the marinade. Choose a shallow flameproof casserole, or a lidded frying-pan large enough to take the chops. Add just sufficient oil to coat the base and brown the chops well on both sides. Remove the chops from the pan and keep to one side. Wipe the casserole or frying-pan clean with kitchen paper.

Melt the butter, add the onion, and stir.

Cut the carrots into long narrow strips and add, along with the flour; stir well. Blend the water and stock cube and pour into the onion mixture. Bring to the boil, stirring. Arrange the chops on top of the mixture and spoon the marinade over. Cover, and cook in the oven until fork tender – about 1 hour.

To serve, remove the chops and keep them hot. Skim off the fat from juices and reduce juices by boiling. Pour over the chops and garnish. *Serves 2.*

Kotelett mit Pflaumen

A southern German dish, of pork chops casseroled with plums.

4 pork chops
½ lb. fresh plums
1 oz. sugar
Powdered cinnamon

4 cloves
1 glass dry red wine
Salt and pepper

OVEN TEMPERATURE: 350°F (mark 4)

Beef and Kidney Casserole (*see page* 9),
Savoury Ham Spaghetti and Veal
Surprise Casserole (*see page* 29)

Trim the chops free of excess fat and heat the trimmings to extract some fat. Use this to fry the chops until lightly but evenly browned. Stew the plums with sugar and just enough water to prevent the fruit from burning. Pass through a sieve. Put the chops in a shallow heatproof dish in a single layer. Add a pinch of cinnamon and the cloves to the plum purée. Pour over the chops. Add the wine, season with salt and pepper.

Cover and cook for 1 hour, adding a little water if necessary during the cooking. *Serves 4.*

Savoury Ham Spaghetti

4 oz. spaghetti	1 oz. plain flour
4 eggs	¾ pint milk
2 tomatoes	4 oz. cheese, grated
4 oz. ham	Salt and pepper
1 oz. butter	

OVEN TEMPERATURE: 350°F (mark 4)

Cook the spaghetti in boiling salted water and drain well. Hard-boil the eggs, shell and slice. Skin and slice the tomatoes. Chop the ham. Make a white sauce with the butter, flour, and milk, add half the cheese and season. Put alternate layers of spaghetti, tomato, egg, and ham in the casserole (reserving some egg and tomato to garnish). Pour the sauce over and sprinkle the other half of the cheese on top. Cook for 30 minutes, until the top is browned.

Garnish with slices of hard-boiled egg and tomato. *Serves 3–4.*

Saucisses au Vin Blanc

1 lb. chipolata pork sausages	Strip of lemon peel
2 oz. butter	½ level tsp. mustard
1 shallot, skinned and finely chopped	¾ oz. flour
⅓ pint dry white wine	Parsley, chopped
½ lb. cauliflower, trimmed	

OVEN TEMPERATURE: 325°F (mark 3)

Prick the sausages. In a shallow lidded flameproof casserole, fry the sausages in ½ oz. butter for 10 minutes. Shake the pan occasionally to brown evenly. Remove sausages, pour off most of the fat. Gently sauté the shallot for 1–2 minutes, pour over the wine and add the thinly sliced cauliflower, lemon peel, and mustard. Replace sausages, cover with a lid and cook in the oven for about 1 hour.

Blend to a paste 1½ oz. butter and the flour. Remove pan from oven to top of stove and, whilst the juices are bubbling, whisk in the blended flour and butter. Season well. Spoon juices over the sausages. Liberally sprinkle with chopped parsley. *Serves 4.*

Lamb and Parsley Casserole

4 meaty chump ends
4 oz. onion, skinned and sliced
4 oz. carrots, peeled and sliced

Black pepper
½ pint stock (beef stock cube)
1 pkt. parsley sauce mix

OVEN TEMPERATURE: 350°F (mark 4)

Fry chump ends in their own fat till beginning to brown. Drain and put into a casserole. Fry onion in the same fat and add to casserole with the carrots, pepper, and boiling stock. Cover and cook for about 1¾ hours till meat is tender.

Strain off liquor and make up to ½ pint with water. Keep meat warm. Make sauce, using stock instead of milk, according to directions on the packet. Pour over meat and serve. *Serves 4.*

Skillet-Style Lamb

8 small best end of neck cutlets or
    4 chump chops
1 oz. butter
1 tbsp. cooking oil
1 lb. potatoes, peeled and diced
1 medium onion, skinned and sliced

4 tomatoes, skinned and sliced
1 medium cooking apple, peeled and
    sliced
Salt and pepper
1 tbsp. chopped parsley
A 5½-oz. can tomato juice

OVEN TEMPERATURE: 325°F (mark 3)

Trim meat. Melt butter and oil in a large shallow flameproof casserole or a lidded frypan large enough to take the chops and potatoes in a single layer. Fry the chops until evenly browned, lift them from drippings, and keep on one side. Add the onion to the drippings, brown lightly. Toss in the

tomatoes, apple, and potatoes, turning to mix evenly. Season well. Arrange cutlets on top. Stir parsley into tomato juice and pour over the cutlets. Cover tightly and cook in the oven for 1¼ hours. Uncover and cook for a further ¼ hour. *Serves 4.*

Lamb Tombasco

1½ lb. stewing lamb
2 tbsps. corn oil
A 15-oz. can plum tomatoes
½–1 tsp. Tabasco sauce

¼ level tsp. dried rosemary
A 2-oz. pkt. onion soup
¼ pint water
Chopped parsley for garnish

OVEN TEMPERATURE: 350°F (mark 4)

Trim fat from the lamb, and chop the meat

into manageable pieces. Heat the oil and

Lamb and Parsley Casserole

quickly brown the lamb on all sides; remove from pan and keep hot. Add the rest of the ingredients to the pan and stir well. Combine with the meat and cook in a covered casserole in the oven for about $1\frac{1}{2}$ hours.

Serve garnished with chopped parsley and partnered by oven-baked jacket potatoes and thinly sliced carrots. *Serves 4.*

Lamb Chops Madeira

4 thick chump chops (approx. $\frac{1}{2}$ lb. each)
1 oz. butter
4 oz. lean bacon rashers, rinded
4 oz. mushrooms, chopped
$\frac{1}{4}$ level tsp. dried rosemary

1 tbsp. chopped parsley
3 level tbsps. fresh white breadcrumbs
6 tbsps. Madeira
Watercress for garnish

OVEN TEMPERATURE: 350°F (mark 4)

Trim chops and make a slit through the centre of each to make a pocket. Melt $\frac{1}{2}$ oz. butter in a flameproof shallow casserole (just large enough to take the chops in a single layer). Sauté the diced bacon until crisp, add mushrooms and continue to cook until soft. Stir in the rosemary, parsley, and breadcrumbs. Season well. Divide this stuffing in four and use one portion to stuff each chop. Sew up the slit with fine string or coarse thread. Melt ½ oz. butter in the casserole and brown the chops on both sides. Pour over the Madeira. Cover

tightly and cook in the oven for about 40 minutes.

Skim off fat, bubble juices to reduce, spoon juices over, and garnish with watercress. *Serves 4.*

Summer Lamb Casserole

2 lb. neck of lamb
2 level tsps. salt
¼ level tsp. pepper
1 lb. new carrots, scraped and sliced
1 lb. small new potatoes, scraped

A ½-lb. pkt. of frozen peas or fresh shelled peas
1 level tbsp. concentrated tomato paste
Fresh mint, chopped

OVEN TEMPERATURE: 325°F (mark 3)

Place meat in a shallow flameproof casserole. Cover with cold water, bring to the boil. Pour off water, rinse meat. Return to casserole with 1 pint cold water, to which the salt and pepper have been added. Bring to the boil. Add the carrots, cover, and cook in the oven for about 1½ hours until meat is fork tender.

Add the potatoes to the casserole, cover, and cook for a further 20 minutes. Remove meat and strip off flesh, roughly cut, and return to casserole with peas and tomato paste. Adjust seasoning, return to the oven for a further 10–15 minutes. To serve, sprinkle with chopped mint. *Serves 4.*

Lamb Julienne

2 lb. boned shoulder lamb, cubed
3 level tbsps. flour
1 level tsp. curry powder
2 level tsps. salt
Freshly ground black pepper
Oil for frying
1½ pints water or chicken stock
8 small onions, skinned
8 carrots, peeled

CRISPY DUMPLINGS: (Optional)
1½ oz. butter
2 oz. fresh white breadcrumbs
8 oz. self-raising flour
1 level tsp. salt
¼ level tsp. dried onion powder
3 tbsps. corn oil
Milk

OVEN TEMPERATURE: 325°F (mark 3)

Toss the lamb cubes in the sifted flour, curry powder, salt and pepper. Cover the base of a frying-pan with oil. Fry meat until well coloured. Stir in any excess flour. Gradually add water or stock, stirring.

Bring to boil. Turn into a casserole (large enough to take the carrots and dumplings later). Add onions. Cover and cook in the oven for 1 hour.

Cut carrots into long thick matchsticks.

Summer Lamb Casserole

Add to casserole, stir. Add dumplings (if wanted) and continue to cook covered for one hour. *Serves 6.*

Crispy Dumplings: Melt butter in a frying-pan, stir in crumbs and cook gently, stirring frequently, until golden. Sift together flour, salt, and onion powder. Stir in oil and enough milk to give a soft but manageable dough. Shape into balls, coat with crumbs, and arrange in casserole.

Lamb Creole

8 lamb chump ends
A 14-oz. can tomatoes
1 level tsp. dried marjoram

Salt and pepper
8 oz. long-grain rice
Parsley sprigs

OVEN TEMPERATURE: 325°F (mark 3)

Place meat in a 4-pint shallow casserole, in a single layer. (Frozen meat should be thoroughly thawed beforehand.) Pour over the canned tomatoes and sprinkle with marjoram. Season with salt and pepper. Cover and cook for 2 hours.

Cook the rice in the usual way and keep hot. When casserole is ready, shape rice into 8 balls with a greased ice-cream scoop, arrange four on the casserole. Serve the rest separately. If more convenient, serve the rice in a separate dish. Garnish with parsley sprigs. *Serves 4.*

Crusty Irish Stew

Crusty Irish Stew

2 lb. middle neck of mutton
2 lb. potatoes, peeled and sliced
2 large onions, skinned and sliced
2 carrots, peeled and sliced
Salt and pepper

4 oz. self-raising flour
½ level tsp. salt
1 oz. butter
Milk to mix

OVEN TEMPERATURE: 350°F (mark 4)

Wipe meat and cut into neat joints, removing the spinal cord. Place alternate layers of the potatoes, onions, carrots, and meat in an ovenproof dish, seasoning each layer with salt and pepper. Add sufficient water almost to cover. Cover with a lid and cook in the centre of oven for 2½ hours.

Make up the topping by sifting the flour with the salt. Rub in the fat and add sufficient milk to form a fairly soft dough. Roll the mixture into small balls and place on top of the stew. Cook, uncovered, for a further 15–20 minutes, or until the topping is browned. *Serves 6.*

Veal Fricassee

1½ lb. veal, cubed
2 tbsps. corn oil
1 pkt. onion sauce mix
½ pint milk
1 level tbsp. concentrated tomato paste

1 tbsp. lemon juice
1 tbsp. sherry
4 oz. button mushrooms, quartered
Salt and pepper
2 tbsps. cream

OVEN TEMPERATURE: 350°F (mark 4)

Veal Fricassee

Sauté the veal in oil till beginning to brown. Drain on absorbent paper then transfer to a casserole. Make sauce up with milk according to directions on the packet. Stir in tomato paste, lemon juice, sherry, and mushrooms. Season to taste, pour over the veal, and mix thoroughly. Cover casserole and cook for about $1\frac{1}{4}$ hours till meat is tender. Before serving stir in cream.

To serve, pipe baskets of creamed potatoes round the edge of the casserole. Brown under the grill or in a hot oven. Fill potato baskets with cooked buttered peas. *Serves 4.*

Veal Surprise Casserole

2 lb. stewing veal
Salt and pepper
1 oz. plain flour
1 oz. butter
2 tbsps. olive oil
1 clove of garlic, finely chopped
A 2¼-oz. can of concentrated tomato purée
1 beef bouillon cube

1 pint boiling water
Bay leaf
A pinch of thyme
A pinch of marjoram
12 stoned black olives
¼ lb. mushrooms, sliced
Boiled rice
Stuffed olives and onions to garnish

OVEN TEMPERATURE: 350°F (mark 4)

Cut the veal into cubes, dip in seasoned flour and brown it in the butter and olive oil, together with the garlic. Add the tomato purée and the bouillon cube dissolved in the boiling water, also the herbs and some seasoning. Cook for $1\frac{1}{2}$ hours; half an hour before the end of the cooking time add the stoned olives and mushrooms. *Serves 6.*

Serve with fluffy white rice, garnished with stuffed olives and with glazed onions, which are made in the following way: cook about a dozen small onions in butter in a saucepan with a lid on, shaking occasionally; meanwhile cook together 2 tbsps. soft brown sugar, 2 tbsps. vinegar and 2 tbsps. port until a thick syrup is obtained. When the onions are cooked, put them into this and boil for a few minutes, until they are all well coated.

Veal Paprika

1 oz. butter
1 lb. pie veal
6 oz. onion, skinned and finely chopped
1 level tsp. paprika
1 level tbsp. concentrated tomato paste

¾ pint stock
6 oz. long-grain rice
A 5-fl. oz. carton soured cream
Salt and freshly milled black pepper
Chopped parsley for garnish

OVEN TEMPERATURE: 325°F (mark 3)

Melt the butter in a frying-pan. When on the point of turning brown, add the veal cut into small pieces, fry briskly. Remove meat, add to casserole. Stir in the onion, fry until tender, add paprika and tomato paste. Add stock, pour over veal, cook for about 1 hour or until tender. Add rice; cover and return to oven for a further ½ hour.

Gently heat soured cream in a small pan, fork through rice. Season. Sprinkle with parsley. *Serves 4.*

CHAPTER 2
Casseroled Fish

Break away from the perennial fried fish and chips or grilled cutlets, and try one of these delicious new ways of cooking fish. There are plenty of recipes here to tempt children who otherwise won't eat fish – for instance, try haddock cooked in cider. One cautionary word: don't (as with meat) turn the temperature down and cook the casserole for longer than the given time – the fish tends to dry out and may be spoiled as a result. On the whole, these dishes are quicker to cook than meat casseroles – and often cheaper, too! We think they're well worth sampling.

Tuna and Celery Casserole

1 oz. butter
1 oz. flour
½ pint milk
Salt and pepper
6 oz. cheese, grated

2 7-oz. cans tuna
4 eggs, hard-boiled and sliced
6 sticks of celery
Toasted breadcrumbs

OVEN TEMPERATURE: 350°F (mark 4)

Melt the butter in a small saucepan, add the flour, and cook, stirring, for 1 minute. Add the milk gradually, stirring constantly. Bring to the boil and cook until smooth. Remove from the heat and stir in the seasoning and 4 oz. of the grated cheese. Drain the oil from the tuna fish, place the flesh in a basin and chop slightly. Slice the hard-boiled eggs and celery and arrange in layers in a casserole with the tuna and cheese sauce.

Top with the remaining grated cheese and the breadcrumbs, and cook in the centre of the oven for about 30 minutes, until crisp and golden brown. *Serves 4.*

Chip-Tuna Casserole

2 7-oz. cans tuna
2 level tbsps. plain flour
¼ level tsp. salt
Pepper

2 cups milk
⅓ cup sherry or 2 tsps. Worcestershire sauce
1 cup crumbled potato crisps

OVEN TEMPERATURE: 375°F (mark 5)

Put into a double saucepan 2 tbsps. of the oil from the tuna; gradually stir in the flour, salt, pepper, and milk and cook, stirring, until smooth and thickened. Add the sherry or Worcestershire sauce. Cover the bottom of a greased 1½-quart casserole with a quarter of the potato crisps. Add ⅓ of the tuna, in chunks, then ⅓ of the sauce. Repeat, making 3 layers; top with the rest of the crisps, cover, and bake in the centre of the oven for 20 minutes. Remove the lid and bake in the centre of the oven for 10 minutes or until brown. *Serves 4.*

Haddock and Mushroom Casserole

1½ lb. fresh haddock fillet, cut up
2 small onions, skinned and chopped
2 oz. mushrooms, sliced
A knob of butter
2 level tsps. flour

A medium-sized can tomato juice
A pinch of mixed herbs
Salt and pepper
2 level tsps. sugar

OVEN TEMPERATURE: 350°F (mark 4)

Wash the fish, cut into pieces, and put into a greased ovenproof dish. Fry the onions and mushrooms in the butter, adding the flour when they begin to colour. Add the tomato juice and bring to the boil; add the herbs, seasoning, and sugar and pour over the fish. Cover with greased greaseproof paper and cook in the centre of the oven for 30 minutes. *Serves 4–6.*

Cidered Haddock Casserole

1–1½ lb. haddock or cod fillet, skinned
½ lb. tomatoes, skinned and sliced
2 oz. button mushrooms, sliced
1 tbsp. chopped parsley

Salt and pepper
¼ pint cider
2 tbsps. fresh white breadcrumbs
2 tbsps. grated cheese

OVEN TEMPERATURE: 350°F (mark 4)

Wash the haddock or cod fillet, cut into cubes, and lay these in an ovenproof dish. Cover with the sliced tomatoes and mushrooms, the parsley, and seasonings, and pour the cider over. Cover with foil and bake in the centre of the oven for 20–25 minutes.

Sprinkle with the breadcrumbs and cheese and brown in a hot oven (425°F, mark 7) or under a hot grill. *Serves 4–6.*

Haddock in Seasoned Cream

6 frozen haddock fillets
1½ oz. butter
2 lb. potatoes, parboiled and sliced
½ onion, skinned and grated

⅓ pint single cream
Salt and pepper
Chopped parsley for garnish

OVEN TEMPERATURE: 325°F (mark 3)

Allow the fillets to thaw, discard the skin, lightly season, and roll up. Spread the butter over a shallow casserole dish large enough to take the fish in a single layer.

Arrange the potato slices over the bottom of the casserole dish and place the fish rolls on top. Sprinkle with onion and seasonings. Spoon over the cream. Cover, and cook for about 1½ hours until the potatoes are tender.

Garnish with plenty of chopped parsley. *Serves 6.*

Haddock and Vegetable Hotpot

1 lb. fresh haddock
1 onion, skinned and chopped
4 oz. French beans, prepared
4 oz. cheese, grated

Salt and pepper
A small can tomatoes
2–3 large potatoes, peeled and sliced

OVEN TEMPERATURE: 350°F (mark 4)

Skin the fish and cut into cubes. Place in a casserole and cover with onion, beans, half the cheese, and some seasoning. Add the tomatoes, cover with sliced potatoes, and season again. Bake in the centre of the oven for 1 hour.

Take from the oven, cover with the remaining cheese and brown under the grill. *Serves 4.*

Fish and Bacon Casserole

4 oz. bacon, rinded and cut up
3 onions, skinned and chopped
½ oz. butter
1½ lb. white fish, free of skin and
    bones

Salt and cayenne pepper
1 tsp. Worcestershire sauce
¼ pint tomato sauce
¼ pint water

OVEN TEMPERATURE: 350°F (mark 4)

Fry the bacon and onion in the butter. Put alternate layers of bacon and onion and the fish into a casserole, sprinkling each layer with salt and cayenne pepper. Mix the sauces with the water and pour over the fish. Cover and cook in the centre of the oven for 45 minutes. *Serves 6.*

Cider Fish Casserole

1½ lb. fillet of cod or haddock
2 onions, skinned and finely chopped
½ lb. tomatoes, skinned and sliced
¼ pint dry cider

1 level tsp. dried sage or mixed herbs
Salt and pepper
2–3 tbsps. fresh white breadcrumbs
1 oz. cheese, grated (optional)

OVEN TEMPERATURE: 325°F (mark 3)

Wash the fish, cut into 4 pieces, and place in a casserole. Sprinkle the onion and tomatoes over and pour the cider around the fish. Sprinkle with the herbs and seasoning, cover with a lid or foil, and bake in the centre of the oven for 20–30 minutes, until tender. Remove the lid, sprinkle the fish with the crumbs and cheese (if used), and brown under a hot grill before serving. *Serves 4.*

Mixed Fish Casserole

1 lb. onions, skinned and chopped
3 tbsps. olive oil
2 cloves garlic, grated
2 green peppers, cut in strips
1 lb. tomatoes, skinned and sliced
½ lb. cod steaks

½ lb. filleted mackerel
½ lb. filleted hake
1 oz. long-grain rice, washed
Salt and pepper
2 tsps. lemon juice or wine vinegar

OVEN TEMPERATURE: 350°F (mark 4)

Fry the onions slowly in the hot oil, add the garlic, peppers, and tomatoes; cover closely and cook slowly in the centre of the oven or on top of the stove until a thick sauce is obtained – about 1½ hours. Add the prepared fish, cut into neat pieces, and the rice. Season well and continue cooking until fish and rice are tender. Finally, add 2 tsps. lemon juice or wine vinegar and serve hot, or allow to cool and serve with salad. *Serves 6.*

Plaice and Mushroom Hotpot

Fish and Macaroni Casserole

2 oz. macaroni (weight before
    cooking)
1½ lb. filleted cod
Salt and pepper
2 tsps. chopped parsley

2 oz. fresh white breadcrumbs
½ pint milk
1 egg, beaten
Butter

OVEN TEMPERATURE: 375°F (mark 5)

Boil the macaroni in salted water until just tender – about 15 minutes. Put the cod in a greased casserole, season well, and add the parsley. Arrange the macaroni and breadcrumbs in layers around the cod.

Heat the milk, add the egg, and pour over the macaroni. Put a knob of butter on top, cover, and bake in the centre of the oven for 1 hour, removing the lid before the end to let the top brown. *Serves 4.*

Plaice and Mushroom Hotpot

2 medium-sized plaice
1 oz. butter
1 oz. flour
¾ pint milk and fish liquor

Salt and pepper
½ lb. mushrooms, peeled
1 lb. parboiled potatoes

OVEN TEMPERATURE: 350°F (mark 4)

Fillet and skin the fish and wash the fillets. Cover the fish bones with water and cook for 15 minutes. Melt the butter, add the flour, cook for 1–2 minutes then stir in the liquid gradually. Bring to the boil for 5 minutes, then season. Cut the fillets in half and put a layer of fish at the bottom of a

casserole, next the mushrooms, then the rest of the fish. Pour the sauce over and cover with the potatoes, cut in half. Put the lid on and cook in the centre of the oven for ¾–1 hour. When the hotpot is half-cooked, remove the lid to allow the potatoes to brown. *Serves 4.*

Spanish Whiting

1 lb. filleted whiting
2 Spanish onions, skinned and sliced
1½–2 tbsps. olive oil
2 tsps. vinegar
A few peppercorns

Salt and pepper
1 lb. tomatoes, skinned and sliced
2 tbsps. chopped celery
½ pint fish stock or water

OVEN TEMPERATURE: 400°F (mark 6)

Wipe the fillets. Boil the onions for about 10 minutes, then drain (reserving the

liquor) and put them in an ovenproof dish with the oil, vinegar, whiting, and peppercorns. Season well, cover with the tomatoes and celery, and pour the stock and 2–3 tbsps. onion water over the fish. Cover the casserole and cook in the centre of the oven for 40 minutes, or until the fish is tender. *Serves 4.*

Turbot with Crab Sauce

4 pieces of turbot or halibut (about 1½ lb.)
2–3 slices of onion
A few sprigs of parsley
½ a bay leaf
Salt and pepper

¼ pint dry white wine
¾ oz. butter
2 level tbsps. flour
¼ pint milk (approx.)
A 3¼-oz. can of crabmeat
1–2 oz. Parmesan cheese, grated

OVEN TEMPERATURE: 350°F (mark 4)

Wash and trim the fish, place in a shallow ovenproof dish with the onion, parsley, bay leaf, and seasoning, and pour in the wine. Cover, and bake in the centre of the oven until tender – about 20 minutes, depending on the thickness of the fish. Drain off and retain the cooking liquid; keep the fish warm. Melt the butter, stir in the flour, and cook for 2–3 minutes. Remove the pan from the heat and gradually stir in the cooking liquid, made up to ½ pint with milk. Bring to the boil and continue to stir until the sauce thickens. Add the flaked crabmeat and continue cooking for a further 2–3 minutes. Place the fish in an ovenproof dish, pour over the sauce, sprinkle with cheese, and brown under the grill. *Serves 4.*

Devonshire Cod with Mushrooms

1 lb. cod fillet
Salt and pepper
1 tomato, skinned and sliced
2 oz. mushrooms, chopped
A small bottle of cider

Butter
¾ oz. flour
Creamed potatoes
1–2 oz. cheese, grated
Sliced tomato and parsley to garnish

OVEN TEMPERATURE: 375°F (mark 5)

Cut the cod into small pieces and put it into an ovenproof dish, with a sprinkling of salt and pepper, the tomato, and the mushrooms. Almost cover the fish with cider and dot the top with shavings of butter. Cover with a piece of greaseproof paper and bake in the centre of the oven for about 30 minutes. Strain off the liquor and use it to make a sauce, with ¾ oz. butter and flour; season to taste and pour over the fish. Pipe creamed potatoes around the edge of the dish and sprinkle the fish with grated cheese.

Garnish with slices of tomato and brown in the oven for 10–15 minutes. Garnish with parsley before serving. *Serves 4.*

Cod and Prawn Casserole

4 frozen cod steaks
A 10¾-oz. can condensed mushroom
   soup
Salt and pepper

2 oz. frozen prawns
2 rounded tbsps. grated Parmesan
   cheese

OVEN TEMPERATURE: 350°F (mark 4)

Place a single layer of cod steaks in a casserole. Empty the can of soup over these and season well. Scatter the prawns on top and sprinkle on the Parmesan cheese. Cover and cook for 45–50 minutes if fish is still frozen or 30–35 minutes if the fish has thawed. *Serves 4.*

Halibut Cutlets Papillotes

Butter
6 halibut or haddock cutlets approx.
   6 oz. each
Salt and freshly ground black pepper
1 lemon
1 lb. firm tomatoes, blanched,
   skinned and seeded

2 oz. fresh white breadcrumbs
2 oz. mature Cheddar cheese, finely
   grated
Chives for garnish

OVEN TEMPERATURE: 325°F (mark 3)

Lightly butter 6 sheets of foil large enough to envelop each cutlet. Lay the fish on the foil, dot with more butter, season with salt and pepper, and squeeze the juice from half a lemon over the fish. Cut the tomato flesh into large dice and spoon this equally over the fish. Package, then place on baking sheets and cook in the oven for about ½ hour. Meanwhile blend together the breadcrumbs and cheese. Season lightly. Unwrap the fish and position on a flameproof serving dish. Spoon over the cheese and breadcrumbs and dot with butter. Flash under a hot grill until golden.

Top with lemon slices cut from the other half of the lemon and sprinkle with snipped chives. *Serves 6.*

Finnish Herring and Potato Casserole

2 large salt herrings
1 lb. boiled potatoes, sliced
1 tbsp. chopped onion or spring onion
2 tbsps. melted butter

1 pint milk
3 eggs, beaten
½ level tsp. pepper
1 oz. dried breadcrumbs

OVEN TEMPERATURE: 350°F (mark 4)

Herrings Braised in Wine

Soak the fish for 6 hours, skin and bone them, and cut in long strips. Butter a baking dish and put in a layer of potato, then one of herring, with a little onion; repeat, finishing with a potato layer, and pour melted butter on top. Add the milk and pepper to the eggs, pour into the baking dish, and sprinkle with breadcrumbs. Bake in the centre of the oven for 30–40 minutes, or until browned. *Serves 4.*

Canned salmon may be used instead of salt herring.

Herrings Braised in Wine

½ bottle Mâcon (red)
Thick slices of onion, carrot, and
  celery
Bay leaf
Bouquet garni

6 peppercorns
Salt and pepper
6 herrings, cleaned
Sautéd button mushrooms and small
  onions and parsley to garnish

OVEN TEMPERATURE: 325°F (mark 3)

Place the wine, sliced vegetables, herbs, peppercorns, and seasoning in a saucepan. Cover and simmer for 30 minutes. Arrange herrings in a single layer in a heatproof dish. Strain the liquor over them, adding a little water if necessary, till nearly covered.

Cover, and cook for 1 hour or more if desired.

Serve the herrings in the liquor, garnished with sautéd mushrooms, small onions, and parsley. *Serves 6.*

Chicken, Duck, and Turkey

The versatile chicken comes into its own when casseroles are on the menu. Here you'll find a dozen different ways of cooking chicken, quite apart from tempting recipes for duck and turkey. If you use a frozen bird, do make sure it has thawed thoroughly before you start cooking. And remember – you can often adapt a favourite recipe to use leftovers from the Sunday roast.

Chicken Chusan

4 large wing or leg chicken portions, halved
2 tbsps. corn oil
½ lb. sausage meat
½ oz. butter
1 medium onion, skinned and chopped

1 pkt. mushroom sauce mix
6 tbsps. milk
4 tbsps. white wine
4 tomatoes, skinned, seeded, and chopped

OVEN TEMPERATURE: 350°F (mark 4)

Fry the chicken in oil till light golden brown. Drain, then place in a casserole. Shape the sausage meat into small balls and fry until evenly coloured. Drain and add to the chicken. Melt the butter in a clean saucepan and sauté onion until soft. Sprinkle in the sauce mix and stir in the milk and wine. Bring to the boil and cook for 2 minutes. Add the tomatoes and pour over the chicken. Cover, and cook for about 1 hour till chicken is tender. *Serves 6.*

Chicken and Walnuts

A 3½–4 lb. roasting chicken, jointed
2 tbsps. sherry
2 level tsps. caster sugar
3 tbsps. oil
8 oz. button mushrooms, washed and sliced

A 6-oz. can water chestnuts, drained and diced (optional)
1 pint chicken stock
2 level tbsps. cornflour
4 oz. halved walnuts
1 oz. butter

OVEN TEMPERATURE: 350°F (mark 4)

Place the chicken in a dish, pour the sherry and caster sugar over it, and leave to marinate for 1–2 hours. Heat the oil in a frying pan and brown the drained chicken pieces. Place the mushrooms and chestnuts in a large casserole. Arrange the chicken pieces on top, pour the chicken juices and chicken stock into the casserole, cover, and bake in the centre of the oven for 2 hours. Drain off the liquor, keep the chicken hot, and thicken the liquor with the cornflour. Brown the walnuts in melted butter for 4–5 minutes and drain.

Dish up the chicken and vegetables, pour

some of the gravy over them and garnish with the browned walnuts. Serve the remaining gravy separately in a jug. *Serves 6.*

Casseroled Chicken and Rice

6–8 oz. long-grain rice
A 4-lb. boiling chicken, jointed and
   skinned
1 pimiento, sliced
2 sticks of celery, scrubbed and
   chopped

½ pint chicken stock or soup
2–3 tbsps. white wine (optional)
3 cloves
Bay leaf
Salt and pepper

OVEN TEMPERATURE: 350°F (mark 4)

Par-boil the rice for 5 minutes, then put alternate layers of rice, chicken, pimiento, and celery in a greased ovenproof dish. Heat together the stock, wine, cloves and bay leaf and pour over the chicken. Check the seasoning. Cover with a lid and cook in the oven for 2½ hours. *Serves 6–8.*

Duckling with Pineapple

2 3½-lb. ducklings
2 medium onions, skinned
4 cloves
Flour
2 tbsps. corn oil
1½ oz. butter
1 level tbsp. ground
   ginger
2 tbsps. clear honey

A 15-oz. can crushed pineapple,
   drained
8 cocktail cherries, stoned
1 chicken stock cube
2 level tbsps. cornflour
Juice of ½ lemon
4 tbsps. brandy
Parsley, chopped

OVEN TEMPERATURE: 325°F (mark 3)

Portion each duckling into 8, skin and truss joints. Make stock with giblets, 1 onion stuck with cloves, and water to cover. Simmer, covered, for ¾ hour. Dredge joints with flour. In a large shallow pan heat oil and butter, add joints flesh side down. Fry for 10 minutes until golden, then place in a large casserole. Finely chop the remaining onion and add to reheated pan juices; sauté. Add ginger, honey, pineapple, and cherries. Crumble cube into 1 pint strained giblet stock. Blend cornflour with a little pineapple juice, and add with the stock and lemon juice to pan juices. Bring to boil, stirring. Pour over duck, cover, and cook for about 2 hours.

Remove excess fat from casserole. Flame brandy and pour into the casserole. Stir, add parsley. *Serves 8.*

Duckling with Peach Sauce

A 4-lb. oven-ready duckling or duck
1 tbsp. oil
1 oz. butter
Salt and pepper
½ pint dry white wine

Sprig of fresh rosemary
3 fresh, firm peaches
1 tbsp. brandy
2 level tsps. arrowroot
Fresh rosemary sprigs

OVEN TEMPERATURE: 325°F (mark 3)

Halve the duckling, trim off excess fat. In a large shallow flameproof casserole, heat oil and butter. Fry duckling for 10 minutes to brown. Remove the bird, pour off fat and wipe casserole. Replace duckling in pan, season well. Pour over the wine, add a sprig of rosemary. Halve peaches, remove stones, but do not peel. Arrange on the duckling. Cover tightly and cook for ½ hour. Remove skin from 4 peach halves, reserve 2 halves, unpeeled, for garnish. Replace skinned peaches in the casserole and con-tinue to cook for a further 1½ hours. Lift duckling from pan juices, keep warm, dis-card rosemary. Lay sheets of absorbent paper over juices to absorb as much fat as possible. Discard paper. Pour brandy into a ladle, gently warm, and flambé; pour into juices. Blend arrowroot with a little water, stir into bubbling juices, and bring to the boil. Replace duckling. Peel and slice remaining peach halves and add to casserole. Garnish with fresh rosemary sprigs. *Serves 4.*

Duck and Orange Casserole

A duckling, jointed
Seasoned flour
½ oz. fat
2 onions, skinned and chopped
¼ lb. mushrooms, sliced

1–2 oz. flour
¾ pint stock
¼ pint orange juice
1 orange, washed

OVEN TEMPERATURE: 350°F (mark 4)

Coat the duck joints with the seasoned flour and fry in the fat for 8–10 minutes, until well browned. Transfer to a casserole. Fry the onions and mushrooms lightly in the hot fat, remove from the pan, and add to the casserole. Stir the flour into the remain-ing fat and brown over a very low heat, stirring all the time. Remove from the heat, gradually stir in the stock and orange juice, and bring to the boil; continue to stir until it thickens. Pour over the duck, cover, and cook in the centre of the oven for about 1 hour.

Pare off the coloured part of the orange rind with a vegetable peeler and cut it into very thin strips. Divide the orange itself into segments, removing any pith or pips. Simmer the strips of rind in water until tender—about 5 minutes; drain well, and sprinkle over the cooked duck joints. Garnish with the orange segments before serving. *Serves 4.*

Duck in Red Wine

A duckling (about 5–6 lb.)
½ clove of garlic, skinned and crushed
2 oz. flour
¾ pint red wine
2 oz. mushrooms, washed and sliced
Bay leaf
Sprigs of parsley
½ level tsp. dried thyme
1 level tsp. salt
1 lb. small onions, skinned
1 lb. small carrots, scraped

OVEN TEMPERATURE: 350°F (mark 4)

Remove the skin and fat from the duck and put them with the giblets into a pan, cover with water, and simmer for 1 hour. Skim off the fat from the surface and let the stock cool. Cut the duck into joints. Heat 2 tbsps. of the duck fat in a pan, then brown the duck joints on all sides. Remove them from the fat and put in a casserole. Add the crushed garlic to the fat, fry for 1 minute and stir in the flour. Add the wine, mushrooms, herbs, and salt. Bring to the boil, stirring constantly until the sauce thickens.

Put the prepared onions and carrots into the casserole, pour the sauce over, cover, and cook in the centre of the over for ¾–1 hour, until tender. *Serves 5–6.*

Turkey and Cranberry Casserole

2 medium-sized onions, skinned and chopped
2 oz. butter or dripping
½ lb. mushrooms, washed and sliced
½ lb. cooked turkey, diced
4 oz. cooked ham, diced
4 oz. leftover stuffing
2 tbsps. chopped parsley
A pinch of thyme
Salt and pepper
4 oz. long-grain rice
2 level tsps. curry powder
½ pint chicken stock
4 oz. cranberry sauce (or jelly)

OVEN TEMPERATURE: 350°F (mark 4)

Sauté the onions in 1 oz. butter until tender. Add the mushrooms and sauté for 2 minutes. Put into a casserole and add the turkey, ham, crumbled stuffing, herbs, and seasoning in layers. Brown the rice in a pan with the remaining butter and the curry powder; add to the casserole and pour in the stock. Cook in the centre of the oven for about 30 minutes, or until the rice is tender and the liquid absorbed.

Garnish with the cranberry sauce (or jelly) arranged in a border round the dish. *Serves 3.*

Chicken Sous La Cloche

1 small chicken, drawn and trussed
¼ pint white wine
¼ pint chicken stock
4 oz. mushrooms, sliced
Salt and pepper
Bay leaf

1½ oz. butter
1½ oz. flour
½ pint milk
Cooked asparagus tips (fresh or
  canned)

OVEN TEMPERATURE: 350°F (mark 4)

Place the chicken in a casserole and add the wine, stock, mushrooms, a little salt, and a bay leaf. Cover and cook in the centre of the oven for about 1¼ hours or until tender. Drain off the liquid – it should make about ½ pint – and retain the mushrooms. Melt the butter, add the flour, stir over a low heat for 1–2 minutes to make a roux, then gradually stir in the milk and the chicken liquid. Bring to the boil, season well, add the asparagus and mushrooms, and boil gently for 2–3 minutes. Remove trussing string from chicken and pour sauce over. *Serves 4.*

Poulet à l'Orange

4 chicken portions, halved
2 tbsps. corn oil
1 pkt. white sauce mix

½ pint milk
2 medium oranges
Black olives

OVEN TEMPERATURE: 375°F (mark 5)

Sauté chicken pieces in oil till well browned. Remove from pan and place in a 4-pint casserole. Make up sauce according to directions on the packet, using ½ pint milk. Thinly pare rind (free from pith) from 1½ oranges and cut in wafer thin strips. Add to the sauce together with the juice of 1 orange. Pour over the chicken. Cover and cook for about ¾ hour till chicken is tender.

Cut remaining orange in slices and use for garnish together with black olives. *Serves 4.*

Chicken Hotpot

4 pieces of chicken
Seasoned flour
2 oz. fat
1 onion, skinned and chopped
2-3 rashers of bacon
½ lb. peas

½ lb. carrots, scraped and sliced
4 tomatoes, skinned and sliced
2 oz. Patna rice
Salt and pepper
¼ pint chicken stock
2-3 oz. frozen prawns

OVEN TEMPERATURE: 375°F (mark 5)

Poulet à l'Orange

Dip the chicken pieces in seasoned flour and fry until golden brown in the hot fat; put on a plate. Sauté the onion until golden. Rind and dice the bacon. In a basin mix together the onion, bacon, peas, carrots, tomatoes, and rice; add the seasoning.

Arrange this mixture and the chicken pieces in layers in a casserole, then pour the stock over. Cover and cook for 1 hour in the oven. Ten minutes before serving add the prawns. *Serves 4.*

Sweet-sour Chicken

4 large chicken joints, halved and
  skinned
2 tbsps. oil
½ pint chicken stock
2 oz. green pepper, seeded and sliced
2 oz. red pepper, seeded and sliced
An 8-oz. can pineapple pieces

2 level tbsps. cornflour
1 tbsp. soy sauce
2 tbsps. chilli vinegar
6 tbsps. wine vinegar
1 level tbsp. black treacle
Salt and pepper
Freshly boiled rice

OVEN TEMPERATURE: 350°F (mark 4)

Quickly fry chicken in hot oil until brown. Transfer to a casserole, pour stock over (this can be made with stock cube). Cover, and cook in the oven for 45 minutes. Pour off the stock into a saucepan. Add peppers and pineapple together with juice and simmer for 5 minutes.

Meanwhile return chicken to oven and keep warm. Blend cornflour with soy sauce, vinegar, and treacle, add to stock, stirring, until thickened and transparent. Adjust seasoning. Pour over chicken. Serve in a ring of rice. *Serves 4.*

Pineapple Chicken Casserole

A small chicken (jointed) or 4 chicken joints
1 oz. seasoned flour
2 oz. butter
¼ pint stock and pineapple juice

An 8-oz. can of pineapple chunks
2 thin slices of lemon
4 oz. blanched almonds, chopped and toasted

OVEN TEMPERATURE: 350°F (mark 4)

Trim the chicken and dredge it with seasoned flour. Melt the butter and brown the chicken well on both sides. Place it in a casserole with the stock and pineapple juice, cover, and bake for about ½ hour in the centre of the oven. Remove from the oven and add the pineapple and lemon. Cover and replace in the oven for another 15 minutes; test for tenderness.

Sprinkle the almonds over the chicken and cook uncovered for 5 minutes, until lightly browned. *Serves 4.*

Pineapple Chicken Casserole

Pollo à la Catalana

A 3-lb. oven-ready weight chicken
Seasoned flour
2 oz. butter
2 tbsps. vegetable oil
12 small onions, skinned
½ oz. flour
½ pint chicken stock

2 tbsps. white wine (optional)
2 level tsps. concentrated tomato paste
Salt and pepper
12 chestnuts
½ lb. chipolata sausages
Fried bread for garnish

OVEN TEMPERATURE: 350°F (mark 4)

Cut chicken in 8 portions, dip each in seasoned flour. Heat butter and oil in a frying-pan, add chicken, and brown well. Remove from the fat and drain. Brown the onions in the fat, then place in the base of a 3½–4-pint casserole. Sprinkle the flour over the drippings in the pan, stir in the chicken stock, white wine, and tomato paste. Place the chicken joints on the onions and pour over the thickened stock. Cover the casserole and cook in the oven for 1 hour.

Meanwhile, prepare and cook the chestnuts. Fry the sausages and cut each into three. Add the chestnuts and sausage to the chicken for about 10 minutes before the end of cooking time. Thicken the gravy slightly if necessary. Garnish with fried bread. *Serves 4–6.*

Chicken Chasseur

4 joints of chicken
1 level tbsp. seasoned flour
1 tbsp. oil
1 oz. butter
1 onion, skinned and chopped
2 oz. mushrooms, washed and sliced

2 tomatoes, skinned, seeded, and diced
¼ pint Espagnole sauce
2 tbsps. white wine
Salt and pepper
Chopped parsley for garnish

OVEN TEMPERATURE: 350°F (mark 4)

Coat the chicken joints in seasoned flour and fry in the oil and butter for about 5 minutes, until golden brown. Remove the chicken joints from the pan and put into a casserole. Fry the onion and mushrooms in the oil and butter for 5 minutes, until golden brown; add the tomatoes, Espagnole sauce, wine, and seasoning, and pour over the chicken joints. Cover, and cook in the centre of the oven for ¾–1 hour until tender.

Place the chicken joints on a serving dish, pour the sauce over them, and sprinkle with parsley. *Serves 4.*

ESPAGNOLE SAUCE:

1 oz. streaky bacon, diced
1 oz. butter
1 shallot, skinned and chopped (or a small piece of onion)
1 oz. mushroom stalks, washed and chopped
1 small carrot, peeled and chopped

¾–1 oz. (2–3 level tbsps.) flour
½ pint beef stock
Bouquet garni
2 level tbsps. concentrated tomato paste
Salt and pepper
1 tbsp. sherry (optional)

Fry the bacon in the butter for 2–3 minutes, add the vegetables, and fry for a further 3–5 minutes until lightly browned. Stir in the flour, mix well, and continue frying until it turns brown. Remove from the heat and gradually add the stock (which can be made from a stock cube), stirring after each addition. Return the pan to the heat and stir until the sauce thickens; add the bouquet garni, tomato paste, and salt and pepper. Reduce the heat and allow to simmer very gently for 1 hour, stirring from time to time to prevent it sticking. Alternatively, cook in the centre of the oven at 325°F (mark 3) for 1½–2 hours.

Strain the sauce, reheat, and skim off any fat, using a metal spoon. Re-season if necessary. One tbsp. sherry may be added just before the sauce is served, if wished.

Chicken Provençal

4 tbsps. oil
8 chicken portions
3 oz. butter
4 onions, skinned and sliced
2 cloves garlic, skinned and crushed
3 oz. flour

8 tbsps. tomato ketchup
1 pint stock (or ½ wine, ½ stock)
Salt and pepper
Worcestershire sauce
½ lb. button mushrooms, sliced

OVEN TEMPERATURE: 375°F (mark 5)

Heat the oil in a pan and fry the chicken until golden brown. Drain, and place in a casserole dish. Melt the butter, sauté the onions and garlic until clear. Stir in the flour, then add tomato ketchup. Cook for 1 minute. Slowly stir in the stock, bring to the boil, and boil for 2 minutes. Add all the other ingredients. Pour over the chicken, cover, and cook for 1½ hours or until chicken is tender. *Serves 8.*

CHAPTER 4
Liver, Kidney, etc.

For casseroling both kidneys and liver, the cheaper ones – ox, and pig's – are the best. They improve with slow cooking and impart a really good flavour to the gravy. Also in this chapter are recipes for cooking other parts of the animal which usually come under the heading 'offal' – and if you follow our instructions, you'll soon have even the fussiest eater in your family enjoying these economical and delicious meals.

Queue de Boeuf Aux Olives Noires

2 oxtails
Cold water
2–3 tbsps. olive oil
6 tbsps. brandy, warmed
¼ pint dry white wine
Stock or water
Bouquet garni, comprising:
   bay leaves

thyme
parsley
orange peel
clove of garlic, crushed
½ lb. black olives, stoned
12–16 oz. long-grain rice

OVEN TEMPERATURE: 300°F (mark 2)

Ask the butcher to chop oxtails into serving-size pieces.

A day ahead

Place in a bowl, cover with cold water, and leave for 2 hours. Drain, dry oxtail on kitchen paper. Heat the oil in a frying pan or, better still, a flameproof casserole. Seal a few pieces of meat at a time. If the frying-pan is used, transfer contents to a casserole. Pour brandy over the oxtail and ignite. When flames have died down, add the wine and let it bubble rapidly for a few minutes. Add just sufficient stock or water to cover; add bouquet garni. Cover, and cook in the oven for 3 hours. Pour the liquor off the meat into a bowl. Remove bouquet garni. Keep liquor and meat separately in the refrigerator overnight.

On the day

Remove fat from the liquor. Bring liquor to the boil and pour over the oxtail in the casserole. Add olives, cover, and cook on top of the stove for another 1–1½ hours until meat comes easily away from the bones. Thicken juices with flour worked together with butter. Serve with a separate dish of boiled rice. *Serves 6–8.*

Baked Stuffed Liver

1 lb. liver
Seasoned flour
Forcemeat stuffing (see page 70)

6–8 small pieces of streaky bacon
¼ pint stock or gravy
Parsley for garnish

OVEN TEMPERATURE: 375°F (mark 5)

Wash and dry the liver, cut it into 6–8 slices. Dip slices in seasoned flour and lay them in a greased baking tin. Put a little stuffing on each piece of liver and lay a piece of bacon on top. Pour the stock round, cover the baking tin with a lid or with greased greaseproof paper and bake in the oven until the liver is tender – about 40 minutes.

Arrange on a hot dish, pour the stock over, and garnish with parsley. *Serves 4.*

Liver en Papillote

For each person:
  2 slices lamb's liver
  1 oz. onion, finely chopped
  1 rasher bacon, rinded and finely cut

  2 mushrooms, sliced
Salt and pepper
Worcestershire sauce
Frozen peas

OVEN TEMPERATURE: 350°F (mark 4)

Place the liver on a piece of buttered foil on a baking sheet. Top with onion, bacon, and mushrooms. Season, and add a portion of frozen peas alongside. Package loosely and cook for about ½ hour in the oven.

Liver Casserole

1 lb. liver
Seasoned flour
6 rashers of bacon
4 onions, skinned

2 oz. lard or dripping
A 12½-oz. can tomatoes
1 tbsp. Worcestershire sauce
8 oz. freshly boiled rice

OVEN TEMPERATURE: 350°F (mark 4)

Wash the liver and remove any skin or tubes; cut it into even-sized pieces and coat with seasoned flour. Cut up the bacon and slice the onions. Fry the liver, bacon, and onions in the hot fat till just brown, then put into a casserole and add the tomatoes and Worcestershire sauce. Cook in the oven for 45 minutes or until the liver is tender and the sauce reduced. Spoon rice round the edge; serve rice separately. *Serves 4.*

Liver and Thyme Casserole

1½ lb. even-sized old potatoes
1 lb. ox liver, sliced
2 level tsps. thyme
Salt and pepper

½ lb. onions, skinned and thinly sliced
Juice of ½ lemon
½ pint water

OVEN TEMPERATURE: 325°F (mark 3)

Belgian Carbonnade (Les Carbonnades
Flamandes – *see page* 57), Moussaka (*see
page* 88) and Liver Casserole

Peel and evenly slice the potatoes. Put half in the base of a 4-pint shallow casserole. Wash liver, remove any skin. Cut slices into 2-in strips. Lay half the liver on top of the potatoes, sprinkle with half the thyme and seasoning. Cover with half the onions, then remaining liver, thyme, and seasoning, then the rest of the onions. Lastly arrange the remaining potatoes in a neat layer. Add the seasoning. Add lemon juice to the water and pour evenly over the sliced potatoes.

Cover and cook in the centre of the oven for about 2 hours. *Serves 4.*

Casseroled Kidneys

1 lb. lambs' kidneys
1 oz. lard or dripping
3 small onions, skinned and finely chopped
½ oz. seasoned flour
Salt and pepper

4 rashers back bacon, rinded
¼ pint stock
1½ lb. potatoes, boiled and creamed
Beaten egg or melted butter to glaze
Chopped parsley for garnish

OVEN TEMPERATURE: 350°F (mark 4)

Clean kidneys, halve, remove the cores, and skin. Place in cold water, bring to the boil, and throw away water. Repeat twice. Melt lard in a frying-pan and fry onions until light golden brown. Stir in flour. Place in a casserole. Arrange kidneys on top of onions, season with salt and pepper, and top with small pieces of bacon. Pour stock over. Cover the casserole and cook in the oven for about 30 minutes until kidney is tender. Line a heatproof dish with creamed potatoes, brushed with egg or butter. Brown in the oven at 400°F (mark 6) or under the grill.

To serve, place kidney mixture in the potato-lined dish, sprinkle with chopped parsley. *Serves 4.*

Stewed Ox Kidney

1 lb. ox kidney
1 tbsp. seasoned flour
1½ oz. dripping

1 onion, skinned and sliced
1 pint stock

OVEN TEMPERATURE: 325°F (mark 3)

Wash kidney thoroughly in cold water. Cut into pieces, removing the core with kitchen scissors, and roll the pieces in the seasoned flour. Melt the dripping in a stewpan or flameproof casserole, and when hot fry the kidney and onion together until brown. Add stock, cover, and cook very gently for about 1½ hours either in the oven or on top of the stove. The gravy may be thickened with a little flour blended with water if necessary.

Serve in a border of piped or forked creamed potatoes or boiled rice. *Serves 4.*

Casseroled Kidneys

Braised Kidneys with Tomatoes and Mushrooms

6 sheep's kidneys
$\frac{1}{4}$ lb. skinless sausages
1 oz. fat
2 onions, skinned and sliced
4 oz. button mushrooms, wiped and
  stalked
A 2$\frac{1}{4}$-oz. can concentrated tomato
  purée

$\frac{1}{2}$ pint stock or water
Salt and pepper
Bouquet garni
A little flour (optional)
$\frac{1}{2}$ lb. tomatoes, skinned, quartered,
  and seeded
Watercress to garnish

Skin, halve, and core the kidneys; cut each sausage into 2 or 3 pieces. Melt the fat in a flameproof casserole or deep lidded frypan. Cook kidneys and sausages slowly until brown; keep on one side. To the dripping add the onions, cook until soft, then add mushrooms and cook a few minutes more. Stir in tomato purée and slowly add stock, stirring. Return the kidneys and sausages to casserole or frypan. Season and add the bouquet garni. Bring to the boil, reduce heat, and simmer for 30 minutes.

Discard bouquet garni, thicken the gravy with a little blended flour, or reduce by rapid boiling. Add tomatoes and heat

through for a minute or two. *Serves 4.*

If wished use 1 lb. sliced lamb's liver instead of the sheep's kidneys.

Lyonnaise Tripe

1½ 2 lb. prepared tripe
2 oz. butter
1½ oz. flour
Stock or water
1 level tsp. concentrated tomato paste

Salt and pepper
2 large onions, sliced or chopped
Wine vinegar
Parsley, chopped

Cut the tripe into neat pieces and cook in the hot butter until golden. Sprinkle in the flour to absorb the extra fat, and when it has cooked a little while, add just enough stock or water to cover the tripe. Add the

tomato paste, salt, and pepper, then the onions; cover, and cook gently on top of the stove for 1 hour. Add the wine vinegar and parsley just before serving. *Serves 6.*

Lancashire Tripe and Onions

2 lb. dressed tripe
1 pint milk
1 pint water

4 onions, skinned and sliced
Salt and pepper
1 level tbsp. flour

Cut the tripe into square pieces, place in a saucepan, and cover with cold water. Bring to the boil and throw away the water. Add to the tripe the milk, water, onions, and seasoning.

Simmer for 3 hours. Mix the flour with a little milk and add to the liquid to thicken; return to the boil and add extra seasoning if required. Serve very hot. *Serves 6.*

Casserole of Orange Braised Hearts

1 lb. ox heart, cut in ½-in. slices
½ oz. plain flour
Salt and pepper
2 oz. butter
¼ lb. onions, skinned

2 oz. streaky bacon
½ lb. carrots, peeled
½ pint beef stock (using 1 beef stock cube)
Rind of 1 orange

OVEN TEMPERATURE: 300°F (mark 2)

If frozen, allow heart to thaw completely before starting to prepare.

Trim fat and sinews from meat and cut into ½-in. thick strips. Mix together in a plastic bag the flour, salt, and pepper. Place the meat in the bag with the seasoned flour and toss together until well coated all over. Heat butter in frying-pan. Slice onions and place in the hot butter and fry, turning frequently until golden brown all over. Drain from the fat and place in a 2-pint casserole. Remove the rind from the bacon and cut each rasher in two. Fry for a few minutes and add to the casserole. Fry meat gently until sealed, then add to the casserole with onions and bacon. Cut carrots

into ¼-in. thick slices. Add to the casserole and mix with onions, bacon, and meat. Dissolve the stock cube in hot water. Pour stock onto juices in frying pan, stirring to prevent lumping. Bring to the boil, simmer for 3 minutes, and pour over the casserole. Cover, and cook for 3 hours.

Remove the rind, free of pith, from the orange, using a potato peeler or sharp knife. Cut into fine strips. Add to the casserole. Return to the oven and cook for a further ½ hour. *Serves 2.*

Casserole of Stuffed Hearts

4 sheeps' hearts
4 oz. breadcrumbs
1 oz. chopped suet
1 tbsp. chopped parsley
1 level tsp. mixed herbs
Salt and pepper
Beaten egg

1 oz. dripping
2 onions, skinned and diced
2 carrots, peeled and diced
1 oz. flour
½–¾ pint stock
Creamed potatoes

OVEN TEMPERATURE: 350°F (mark 4)

Wash the hearts thoroughly and cut through the central cavity membrane, to make room for the stuffing. Mix together the breadcrumbs, suet, herbs, salt, and pepper, and bind with beaten egg. Stuff the hearts with this and stitch the top to keep it in place. Melt the dripping, fry the diced vegetables and put these in a cas-

serole. Fry the hearts, then put them on the vegetables. Make a gravy from the remaining fat, with the flour and stock, pour it over the hearts and cook, covered, in the oven for about 2 hours.

Serve with the gravy and creamed potatoes. *Serves 4.*

Casserole of Lambs' Tongues

4 lambs' tongues
1 oz. fat or oil
1 onion, skinned and sliced
1 carrot, peeled and grated

4 large tomatoes, skinned and sliced
1 tbsp. chopped parsley
Salt and pepper
Stock

OVEN TEMPERATURE: 350°F (mark 4)

Wash the tongues and trim if necessary.

Fry the onion in the fat or oil until golden

brown, drain, and place in a casserole. Add the tongues, carrot, tomatoes, parsley, salt and pepper, and pour over just enough stock to cover. Cook in the centre of the oven for about $1\frac{1}{2}$ hours. *Serves 4.*

If preferred, the tongues may be skinned and then reheated in the liquor just before serving.

Devilled Tongue

1 lb. cooked tongue in a thick slice
1 level tbsp. flour
1 tbsp. vinegar
1 tbsp. tomato sauce
$\frac{1}{4}$ level tsp. ground ginger

$\frac{1}{4}$ level tsp. curry powder
$\frac{1}{4}$ level tsp. dry mustard
$\frac{1}{4}$ level tsp. mixed spice
$\frac{1}{2}$ pint stock

OVEN TEMPERATURE: 350°F (mark 4)

Dice the tongue and place in a casserole. Mix together the flour, vinegar, tomato sauce, ginger, curry powder, mustard, and spice to a paste. Gradually add the stock. Pour over the tongue, cover, and cook in the oven for $\frac{1}{2}$ hour. *Serves 3.*

Sweetbread Hotpot

1 lb. sweetbreads
1 onion, skinned and chopped
8 oz. peas
4 oz. mushrooms, sliced
1 oz. butter

2 oz. plain flour
1 pint stock
Salt and pepper
1 tsp. mixed herbs
Toast to garnish

OVEN TEMPERATURE: 325°F (mark 3)

Soak the sweetbreads in salted water until free from blood. Cover with water, bring slowly to the boil, then pour off the liquid. Sauté the onion, peas, and mushrooms slowly for 5 minutes in the butter. Add the flour and stir until cooked. Add the liquid slowly, season, add the herbs, and bring to the boil. Chop the sweetbreads and add. Cook in a warm oven for about 2 hours.

Serve garnished with triangles of toast. *Serves 4.*

CHAPTER 5

Classic Dishes

This chapter gives you a selection of classic dishes from home and abroad that you may have eaten on holiday or in a restaurant, but never ventured to cook in your own home. Some of them are surprisingly simple to make – the most important factor being the organisation needed to leave yourself enough time for the actual cooking. We have also included well known favourites, such as Irish Stew and Lancashire Hotpot. As you might expect with traditional dishes, there are many variations and our recipes may not always tally with other versions you have tried. Make a change and try our recipes – they have all been carefully tested in our own kitchens, are classically sound, and taste delicious!

Les Carbonnades Flamandes

1½ lb. chuck or blade-bone steak
1½ oz. dripping or oil
2 medium-sized onions, sliced
1 clove garlic, crushed
Pinch of powdered thyme
Bay leaf
½ pint brown ale or stout

½ pint stock or water
Salt and pepper
1 oz. butter
1 oz. flour
2 level tsps. sugar
Chopped parsley for garnish

Trim steak and cut in strips or cubes. Melt dripping in a saucepan and seal meat. Lift from pan and put on one side. Fry onions until soft and lightly browned. Add the meat, garlic, thyme, bay leaf, beer, and stock. Season. Bring to the boil, cover, reduce heat, and simmer gently until the meat is tender – about 2 hours. Arrange drained meat in a serving dish, keep warm. Melt butter, gradually work in the flour, cook over low heat for 2–3 minutes. Gradually stir in the meat juice and sugar. Bring to the boil and boil gently for a few minutes; check seasoning. Pour over the meat.

Garnish with parsley and serve with boiled potatoes. *Serves 4.*

Blanquette of Veal

1–1½ lb. lean veal (from shoulder or
   knuckle), cubed
2 onions, skinned and chopped
2 carrots, peeled and chopped
Squeeze of lemon juice
Bouquet garni
Salt and pepper

1 oz. butter
1 oz. flour
1 egg yolk
2–3 tbsps. cream
Lemon wedges and bacon rolls to
   garnish

Put the meat, onions, carrots, lemon juice, bouquet garni, and seasoning into a large pan with enough water to cover. Put on the lid and simmer gently for about 1½ hours until the meat is tender. Strain off the cooking liquid, retaining 1 pint, and keep the meat and vegetables warm. Melt the butter, stir in the flour, and cook for 2–3 minutes. Gradually stir in the pint of cooking liquid, bring to the boil, and boil for 2–3 minutes, stirring all the time. Adjust the seasoning, remove from the heat, and when slightly cooled stir in the egg yolk and cream. Pour over the meat and vegetables and before serving reheat without boiling for a further 5 minutes, to allow the flavours to blend.

Serve with lemon wedges and bacon rolls. *Serves 4.*

Couscous

2 tbsps. corn oil
6 shoulder lamb chops
2 onions, peeled and sliced
2 oz. chick peas, soaked overnight
½ lb. carrots, peeled and sliced
2 turnips, peeled and diced
Salt and pepper
1 pint water
2 oz. stoned raisins
2 oz. blanched almonds, halved
1 lb. courgettes, sliced
2 small green peppers, seeded and
    sliced

A 14-oz. can tomatoes
1 level tsp. paprika pepper
½ lb. ready-bought couscous
1 pint boiling water
1 oz. butter
½ level tsp. salt

HOT PEPPERY SAUCE:
½ pint stock
1 level tsp. Harissa
2 level tsps. concentrated tomato
    paste
Chopped parsley for garnish

Heat oil, and brown the chops. Add onions, peas, carrots, turnips, salt, pepper, and water. Bring to the boil, cover, and simmer for 1 hour. Add raisins, almonds, courgettes, peppers, tomatoes, and paprika and simmer for a further ½ hour till meat is tender. Make up couscous according to packet directions, using water, 1 oz. butter and salt. Blend ½ pint stock from stew with Harissa and tomato paste. Keep hot.

To serve, spread couscous on a large platter, pile stew on top. Sprinkle with parsley. Serve peppery sauce separately. *Serves 6.*

Harissa is a concentrated pepper paste sold in cans.

Osso Buco

2 lb. shin of veal (4 pieces)
Salt and pepper
2 oz. butter
1 medium onion, skinned and finely
    chopped
2 carrots, peeled and thinly sliced
2 stalks celery, thinly sliced
¼ pint dry white wine

1 level tbsp. flour
½ pint stock
¾ lb. tomatoes, skinned and quartered
Pinch of dried rosemary
2 tbsps. chopped parsley
1 small clove of garlic, skinned and
    finely chopped
Grated rind of 1 lemon

OVEN TEMPERATURE: 350°F (mark 4)

Osso Buco

Ask your butcher to saw the veal into 4 1½–2 in. thick slices. Season with salt and pepper. Melt butter in a saucepan large enough to take the veal in one layer. Brown veal, then put aside. If necessary, add a little more butter before gently frying the onion, carrots, and celery until they are just beginning to brown. Pour off excess fat, return the meat to the pan, add the wine. Cover and cook gently for 1 hour. Transfer meat to a large shallow casserole.

Blend flour with a little stock to a smooth paste, stir in remaining stock, and pour round the veal. Add the tomatoes and rosemary, cover and continue to cook gently in the oven for a further hour until the meat is tender. Sprinkle with parsley, garlic, and lemon rind. *Serves 4.*

If convenient, prepare the day before (to the point where meat is transferred to a casserole). Cool quickly and refrigerate.

Irish Stew

1 lb. middle neck of mutton
2 lb. potatoes, peeled
2 large onions, skinned

Salt and pepper
Chopped parsley for garnish

Prepare the meat by wiping thoroughly, removing the marrow and cutting into neat joints. Cut the potatoes and onions in rings

and place alternate layers of the vegetables and meat in a pan, finishing with a layer of potatoes. Add salt and pepper and suffi-

Boeuf Bourguignonne (*above*) and
Coq au Vin (*below*)

cient water to half-cover. Bring to the boil and simmer gently for about 2 hours, or until the meat and potatoes are tender. Pile the meat, gravy, and some of the potatoes in the centre of a hot dish. Place the rest of the potatoes at either end of the dish and sprinkle a little chopped parsley over them. *Serves 4.*

Boeuf Bourguignonne

2 lb. topside of beef
1½ oz. lard
4 oz. thick rashers streaky bacon, rinded
1 level tbsp. flour
¼ pint dry red wine (Burgundy)
¼ pint stock

Pinch of dried thyme
½ bay leaf
1 clove garlic, skinned and crushed
Salt and pepper
6–12 shallots skinned
3 tbsps. brandy (optional)

OVEN TEMPERATURE: 325°F (mark 3)

Trim meat, and cut into large cubes. Melt 1 oz. lard in a frying-pan. Brown meat on all sides, a few pieces at a time. Place meat in a 3½-pint casserole. Dice bacon, add to frying-pan, fry until beginning to colour. Stir in flour and continue to cook until brown, stirring occasionally. Gradually stir in the wine and stock and bring to the boil. Add thyme, bay leaf, crushed garlic, and seasoning to taste. Pour over meat. Cover, and cook in the oven for 2 hours.

Melt ½ oz. lard in a small pan and brown the shallots. Drain. Ignite brandy, and add with shallots to casserole. Reduce heat to 300°F (mark 2) and cook for a further ½ hour until meat is tender. Discard bay leaf before serving. *Serves 6.*

Coq au Vin

A 3-lb. oven-ready chicken
4 oz. streaky bacon rashers, rinded
1 oz. butter
4 small onions, skinned and sliced
4–6 oz. button mushrooms, stalked
Bay leaf

Few parsley sprigs
Pinch of thyme
Salt and pepper
½ pint dry red wine
Beurre manié (¾ oz. flour, ¾ oz. butter)

OVEN TEMPERATURE: 350°F (mark 4)

Prepare the chicken and joint into 8 pieces. Cut bacon into cubes. Melt the butter, fry the bacon and onions until they start to colour, drain, and keep on one side. Fry the chicken until lightly browned, and then transfer chicken and juices to a casserole. Add onions and bacon mixture, whole mushrooms, herbs, and seasoning; add wine. Cover and cook in the oven for 1–1¼ hours until chicken is tender. Strain off

Navarin of Lamb

liquor from casserole into a saucepan. Keep chicken hot. Skim off any fat, and discard bay leaf and parsley sprigs from liquor. Cream together the butter and flour for beurre manié, then whisk into liquor a little

at a time over a low heat. Cook gently for 5 minutes. Adjust seasoning and strain over chicken. Return to oven for 15 minutes. *Serves 4.*

Navarin of Lamb

2 lb. middle neck of lamb
2 oz. lard or dripping
2 level tbsps. flour
2 level tsps. salt
$\frac{1}{4}$ level tsp. pepper
3 level tbsps. concentrated tomato paste

1 pint hot water
Bouquet garni
  (including cut clove of garlic)
4 onions, skinned and sliced
4 carrots, peeled and sliced
4 small turnips, peeled and sliced
8 small potatoes, peeled

Trim meat and cut into serving pieces. Melt 1 oz. fat in a saucepan and brown the meat a few pieces at a time. Dredge with flour seasoned with salt and pepper. Brown again. Gradually stir in the tomato paste and hot water. Add bouquet garni, bring to the boil, reduce heat, cover, and simmer for 1 hour. Melt 1 oz. fat in a pan and fry

vegetables except potatoes; when lightly browned add to the meat, and continue to simmer for a further $\frac{1}{2}$ hour. Discard bouquet garni. Add even-sized potatoes and simmer for a further $\frac{1}{2}$ hour.

Before serving, adjust seasoning and skim off any surplus fat. *Serves 4.*

Chicken Marengo

Chicken Marengo

A 3½-lb. oven-ready chicken
1 oz. lard
Salt
8 oz. mushrooms, stalked and sliced
1 oz. butter

SAUCE:
1½ oz. butter
2 sticks celery, chopped
1 small carrot, peeled and chopped
2 medium onions, peeled and
  chopped

1 rasher bacon, rinded and diced
1 mushroom, chopped
1 tomato, quartered
Sprig of parsley
Blade of mace
Bay leaf
Salt and freshly ground pepper
1½ oz. flour
A 2¼-oz. can concentrated tomato
  purée
1 pint chicken stock
1 tbsp. sherry

OVEN TEMPERATURE: 375°F (mark 5)

If the chicken is frozen, allow to thaw thoroughly, then place in a deep roasting tin. Heat the lard and pour over the chicken. Season skin with salt. Roast for 20 minutes per lb.

Meanwhile make the sauce. Heat the butter in a saucepan; add celery, carrot, onions, bacon, mushroom stalks, tomato, parsley, mace, bay leaf, salt, and pepper. Fry gently, stirring until dark golden brown all over. Add flour and stir well, then add tomato purée. Slowly add stock, stirring constantly to prevent lumps appearing. Add sherry, bring to the boil, stirring.

Cover and simmer for 1 hour. Remove flesh from chicken and cut into manageable pieces. Place in a large casserole. Sauté mushrooms in butter and add to casserole.

Strain sauce over chicken, discarding vegetables. Cover, cook in the oven at 350°F (mark 4) for ½ hour to heat thoroughly. *Serves 6.*

Poulet en Cocotte Bonne Femme

A 4-lb. oven-ready chicken

STUFFING:
    4 oz. sausage meat
    1½ oz. fresh white breadcrumbs
    1 chicken liver, chopped
    2 level tbsps. chopped parsley
Salt

Freshly ground black pepper
3 oz. butter
8 oz. lean back bacon, in one slice
1½ lb. potatoes, peeled
¼ lb. shallots, skinned
1 lb. small new carrots, scraped
Chopped parsley for garnish

OVEN TEMPERATURE: 350°F (mark 4)

Work together the stuffing ingredients. Stuff the bird at the neck end, plump up, and secure with a skewer. Truss as for roasting. Season well. Melt the butter in a large pan, add the chicken and brown all over. Transfer chicken and butter to a large casserole. Rind the bacon and cut in ¾-in. cubes. Add to casserole, cover, and cook in the oven for 15 minutes. Meanwhile cut the potatoes into 1-in. dice. Remove casserole from oven and baste chicken. Surround with potatoes, shallots, and carrots, turning them in the fat. Season. Return to the oven and cook, covered, for a further 1½ hours until chicken and vegetables are tender.

Garnish with chopped parsley. Have a plate to hand for carving the bird. Serve vegetables and juices straight from the casserole. *Serves 6.*

Lancashire Hotpot

2 lb. potatoes
2 lb. mutton (middle neck)
1 onion, skinned
2 kidneys, cored
4–5 mushrooms
1 oz. dripping

1 oz. flour
¾ pint stock
Salt and pepper
1 level tsp. caster sugar
20 oysters (optional)
Parsley

OVEN TEMPERATURE: 350°F (mark 4)

Peel the potatoes and slice them thickly. Cut the meat into chops. Slice the onion and the kidneys; peel and slice the mushrooms. Brown the meat in the hot dripping, then drain and put into a fairly large casserole. Lightly brown the onion, then add the flour and cook until well coloured; mix in the hot stock gradually, stirring all the

Poulet en Cocotte Bonne Femme (*top*) and Lancashire Hotpot (*bottom*)

time, and add the seasoning and sugar. Spread the kidney over the mutton and add a layer of mushrooms and then a layer of oysters, if used. Arrange potatoes overlapping all over the top. Strain the sauce into the casserole, cover, and cook for about $1\frac{3}{4}$ hours in the oven.

Remove the lid and continue cooking for 15 minutes or so until the top is well browned. Garnish with parsley and serve with red cabbage, which is the traditional Lancashire accompaniment. *Serves 6–8.*

Simpler versions of this recipe use just the mutton, omitting the kidneys and oysters, and often the mushrooms also.

Cassoulet (1)

1 lb. dried butter beans
1 lb. streaky salt pork, rinded
$\frac{3}{4}$ lb. shoulder of lamb
2 tbsps. corn oil
$\frac{1}{2}$ lb. onions, skinned and sliced
$1\frac{1}{2}$ lb. leeks, washed and sliced
Bouquet garni consisting of:
    4 parsley stalks
    3 bay leaves
    5 cloves
    pared rind of 1 lemon
    1 level tsp. dried thyme
$\frac{1}{4}$ level tsp. black pepper
$\frac{1}{4}$ lb. garlic sausage (salami)
Chopped parsley for garnish

A day ahead

Soak the beans in enough water to cover them. Take the meat from the bone and dice the pork and lamb into serving-sized pieces. Keep covered in a cool place (preferably a refrigerator) until making up the dish the following day. Chop the bones, place in a pan just covered with water, and simmer gently for about 2 hours. Drain off stock, allow to cool, and remove any fat.

On the day

Heat the oil in a large flameproof pan, brown the meat lightly, and remove from pan. Sauté the onions and leeks in the meat juices for 10 minutes. Reserve a quarter of them on one side. Add the meat, drained butter beans, onions, and leeks to the pan, with the bouquet garni tied in muslin. Pour on 1½ pints bone stock and season well with pepper. Using scissors, snip the garlic sausage into strips and add to the rest of the ingredients. Cover pan tightly and simmer for about 1½–2 hours. Fork the beans through occasionally, to allow them to cook evenly until beans and meat are tender. Add reserved leeks, remove bouquet garni, and serve garnished with chopped parsley. *Serves 6.*

Cassoulet (2)

1 lb. haricot beans, soaked overnight
1 lb. onions, skinned
4 whole cloves
Bay leaf
A ½-lb. piece bacon, rinded and diced
Parsley stalks
A 2½–3 lb. chicken
2 oz. butter

2 cloves garlic, skinned and crushed
½ lb. garlic sausage, skinned and sliced
1 level tsp. dried thyme
Salt and pepper
½ pint milk
Watercress for garnish

OVEN TEMPERATURE: 325°F (mark 3)

Cassoulet with Chicken

Put the drained, soaked, and rinsed beans in a large pan covered with salted water. Add one small onion studded with cloves, bay leaf, bacon rind, and parsley stalks. Simmer, covered, until the beans are tender but not broken up – about $1\frac{3}{4}$ hours. The water should have been absorbed.

Roast the chicken for about $\frac{3}{4}$ hour at 400°F (mark 6). Divide into 8 portions. Fry the remaining sliced onions in butter until golden brown, add garlic. Lightly stir the bacon, sausage, fried onions, and thyme into the beans. Adjust seasoning. Turn into a large (10-pint) casserole and slightly embed the chicken portions into the beans. Pour over $\frac{1}{2}$ pint hot milk. Cover tightly with a lid. Cook in the oven for about 1 hour.

Serve from the casserole with a tomato and watercress salad. *Serves 8.*

CHAPTER 6
Game

'Game' doesn't necessarily mean the exotic (and expensive) pheasant or venison, it's a heading that can also cover hare and the humble rabbit, and we've included recipes for all of them in this chapter. Remember, the older, cheaper birds are a better buy for casseroling than the young ones. Nowadays frozen game birds are generally obtainable throughout the year, so you can have them out of season as well as in.

Hunter's Casserole

A 3½-lb. rabbit (2½-lb. skinned)
Salt and freshly ground pepper
2 tbsps. oil
½ oz. butter

¼ pint dry white wine
1 clove garlic, peeled and crushed
2 tbsps. chopped parsley

OVEN TEMPERATURE: 375°F (mark 5)

Skin and joint the rabbit into small pieces; season. Heat oil and butter in a heavy pan and fry rabbit briskly on all sides until golden brown. Remove from pan and place in a casserole. Drain off fat from pan, add wine, garlic, and parsley, adjust seasoning, and heat for a few minutes. Pour over rabbit, cover tightly, and cook in the centre of the oven for about 45 minutes or until the flesh feels tender when forked.

Remove flesh from bones, return to pan juices and cook for a further 15 minutes. Sprinkle with more chopped parsley and serve with buttered carrot rings and fluffy rice. *Serves 4.*

Brown Casserole of Rabbit

A rabbit, jointed
2 oz. seasoned flour
2 oz. dripping
1 onion or leek, sliced
1 meat cube or 2 tsps. meat extract
1 pint stock or water
2 carrots, peeled and diced

1 stalk of celery, chopped
Bouquet garni
1 tbsp. tomato ketchup
A pinch of ground nutmeg
Forcemeat balls or fried croûtons to garnish

OVEN TEMPERATURE: 350°F (mark 4)

Wash and joint the rabbit and soak in cold salted water to remove the blood. Dry the pieces and toss in seasoned flour, then fry, several joints at a time, until lightly browned. Remove from the pan, add the onion or leek, and fry gently for a few min-utes; add the remaining flour and fry until lightly browned. Add the meat cube or extract with the liquid and stir until boiling. Put the rabbit and the vegetables into a casserole and pour the sauce over. Add the bouquet garni, ketchup, and nutmeg, cover, and cook in the centre of the oven for about 2 hours.

Remove the herbs and serve the cas-serole garnished with forcemeat balls or croûtons. *Serves 4.*

Forcemeat Balls: see page 70.

Sweet-sour Rabbit with Prunes

2 lb. prepared rabbit, jointed
6 oz. onions, skinned and sliced
¼ pint dry white wine
½ pint chicken stock
1 bay leaf
2 tbsps. redcurrant jelly
A few peppercorns

8 whole prunes, stoned
2 oz. seedless raisins (optional)
1 tbsp. malt vinegar
2 level tsps. cornflour
Salt and freshly milled black pepper
Chopped parsley and fried almonds
   for garnish

OVEN TEMPERATURE: 325°F (mark 3)

Sweet-sour Rabbit with Prunes

Marinate the cleaned and jointed rabbit overnight in the onion and wine. Discard onion. Place wine and rabbit in a flame-proof casserole, add chicken stock, bay leaf, redcurrant jelly, and a few peppercorns. Bring to the boil. Submerge prunes and raisins in the liquor. Cover casserole tightly. Cook in the oven for about 1½ hours until rabbit is really tender and prunes plump.

Remove meat and discard bones. Strain liquor into a clean pan, retain prunes and raisins, add the vinegar blended with the cornflour. Adjust seasoning and boil 1–2 minutes.

Arrange rabbit, prunes, and raisins in a clean hot casserole; pour thickened juices over. Garnish with parsley and fried almonds. *Serves 4.*

Jugged Hare

A hare
2 oz. bacon, rinded and chopped
1 oz. lard or dripping
1 onion, skinned and stuck with 2 cloves
1 stick of celery, chopped
1 carrot, peeled and sliced

1½ pints stock
Bouquet garni
Juice of ½ lemon
3 level tbsps. flour
1 tbsp. redcurrant jelly
1 glass of port or red wine (optional)

OVEN TEMPERATURE: 325°F (mark 3)

Prepare the hare, retaining the blood; wipe and joint (your butcher or fishmonger will do this for you). Fry the joints with the bacon in the lard until they are lightly browned (about 2 minutes). Transfer to a deep casserole and add the vegetables, enough stock to cover the joints, the bouquet garni, and lemon juice. Cover and cook in the centre of the oven for 3–4 hours, or until tender.

A few minutes before serving, blend the flour with a little cold water to a smooth cream, stir in the blood of the hare and add to the casserole, with the jelly and wine (if used). Reheat without boiling and serve with redcurrant jelly and forcemeat balls. *Serves 4.*

FORCEMEAT BALLS

2 oz. cooked bacon, finely chopped
2 oz. shredded suet
4 oz. fresh white breadcrumbs
1 tbsp. chopped parsley
1 level tsp. mixed herbs

Grated rind of ½ lemon
1 egg, beaten
Salt and pepper
A little milk or stock

Mix together the bacon, suet, breadcrumbs, parsley, herbs, lemon rind, egg, and seasoning with enough milk or stock to bind the mixture. Roll into small balls and bake in a shallow greased ovenproof dish at 325°F (mark 3) until lightly browned and slightly crisp on the outside – about 20 minutes.

For forcemeat stuffing, blend together as above and use to stuff bird, etc.

Jugged Hare

Hare in Red Wine

A small hare
6 oz. bacon, rinded
2–3 tbsps. dripping
2 oz. flour
1 pint stock or water
½ lb. small onions, skinned

2 cloves
2 bay leaves
2 peppercorns
Salt and pepper
2 glasses of red wine

OVEN TEMPERATURE: 300°F (mark 2)

Cut the hare into small pieces, taking the flesh off the bones where possible. Cut the bacon into thin strips and mix with the hare. Heat the dripping in a thick stewpan and fry the meat, turning it frequently until brown; take it out and keep hot. Stir in the flour and add the stock. Transfer, with the meat, sliced onions, herbs, and seasonings, to a casserole and cook gently towards the bottom of the oven for about 3 hours. Add the wine and continue to cook until the liquor is thick; remove any excess fat.

Serve in the casserole, with a piped border of creamed potato. *Serves 4.*

Tipsy Pigeons

8 black olives
4 tbsps. sherry
2 pigeons, plucked and drawn
2 tbsps. oil
1 large onion, skinned and sliced
4 slices garlic sausage
4 oz. bacon, rinded and chopped
3 level tbsps. flour
½ pint chicken stock
2 tbsps. brandy
Salt and pepper

OVEN TEMPERATURE: 350°F (mark 4)

Marinate the olives in the sherry for 2 hours. Fry the pigeons in the oil until golden brown – about 5 minutes. Remove from the pan with a slotted spoon and put into a casserole. Fry the onion, garlic sausage, and bacon in the remaining fat until golden brown – about 5 minutes. Remove from the pan with a slotted spoon and add to the casserole, with the sherry and olives. Stir the flour into the fat remaining in the pan and cook for 2–3 minutes. Gradually stir in the stock, bring to the boil, and stir until it thickens. Add the brandy, season, and pour the sauce over the pigeons.

Cover, and cook in the centre of the oven for 45 minutes, until tender. *Serves 4.*

Casserole of Pigeon

2–3 pigeons, plucked, drawn, and jointed
2–3 tbsps. oil
2 oz. bacon, rinded and chopped
2 carrots, peeled and sliced
1 onion, skinned and chopped
3 level tbsps. flour
1 pint chicken stock
1 tbsp. concentrated tomato paste
Salt and pepper

OVEN TEMPERATURE: 350°F (mark 4)

Fry the pigeon joints in the oil for about 5 minutes, until golden brown, remove from the pan with a slotted spoon and put into casserole. Fry the bacon, carrots, and onion in the remaining oil for about 5 minutes, until golden brown. Remove the vegetables from the pan with a slotted spoon and add to the casserole. Stir the flour into the remaining fat in the pan and cook for 2–3 minutes. Remove the pan from the heat and gradually stir in the stock. Bring to the boil, continue to stir until it thickens, and add the tomato paste and seasoning. Pour the sauce over the pigeon joints, cover, and cook in the centre of the oven for about ¾–1 hour, or until the pigeon is tender.

Serve in a border of creamed potatoes. *Serves 4.*

Pigeons in Cream

6 pigeons
4 oz. melted butter
¼ pint stock
2 level tbsps. redcurrant jelly

½ pint double cream
Salt and pepper
1 tbsp. brandy
Chopped parsley for garnish

OVEN TEMPERATURE: 325°F (mark 3)

Wash the pigeons and trim away the claws and undercarriage bones with scissors. Fry in the melted butter until well-browned on each side of the breast. Place in a casserole, breast side down into butter and juices; add the stock and cook, tightly covered, in the oven for about 2 hours or until really tender. Remove birds from the casserole and keep warm.

Reduce pan juices by half. Stir in the redcurrant jelly and double cream; adjust seasoning. Bring to the boil, reduce heat, and add the brandy. Flame and pour over the bird. Serve with plenty of chopped parsley. *Serves 6.*

Partridge with Cabbage

2 partridges, plucked, drawn, and
    trussed
Butter or bacon fat
1 medium-sized firm cabbage
4–6 oz. streaky bacon
Salt and pepper

1 carrot, peeled and roughly chopped
1 onion, skinned
2–3 cloves
Bouquet garni
Stock
Smoked sausages (optional)

OVEN TEMPERATURE: 350°F (mark 4)

Fry the partridges in butter or bacon fat until golden brown. Cut the cabbage in quarters, removing the outside leaves and any hard pieces of stalk, wash it well, cook for 5 minutes in boiling salted water, then drain. Line a casserole with the bacon and lay half the cabbage over it, with seasoning to taste. Put the partridges on the top, with the carrot, the onion stuck with the cloves, and the bouquet garni; add the rest of the cabbage and more seasoning. Cover with stock, put on a lid and cook in the centre of the oven for 1–1½ hours, or until the birds are tender.

To serve, remove the partridges and bacon from the casserole and cut the birds into neat joints. Remove the carrot, onion, and bouquet garni and cut the cabbage in shreds with a sharp knife. Serve the cabbage with the pieces of partridge on top of it and the bacon and sausage (if used) around. *Serves 4.*

As a variation, 1–2 lightly fried smoked sausages are sometimes added to the casserole mixture before it is put into the oven.

Casserole of Partridge

2 medium-sized onions, skinned and
  sliced
2 sticks of celery, scrubbed and
  sliced
¼ lb. mushrooms, washed and sliced
4 oz. bacon, rinded and chopped
1 tbsp. oil
1 oz. butter

2 partridges, plucked, drawn, and
  jointed
3 level tbsps. flour
¾ pint stock
A 15-oz. can tomatoes, drained
Salt and pepper
¼ pint red wine

OVEN TEMPERATURE: 350°F (mark 4)

Fry the onions, celery, mushrooms, and bacon in the oil and butter for about 5 minutes, until golden brown. Remove from the pan with a slotted spoon and line the bottom of a casserole with them. Fry the partridge joints in the oil and butter for about 5 minutes, until golden brown. Remove from the pan with the slotted spoon and put in the casserole on the bed of vegetables. Stir the flour into the fat remaining in the pan and cook for 2–3 minutes. Gradually stir in the stock, bring to the boil, and continue to stir until it thickens. Add the tomatoes, salt, pepper, and wine and pour the sauce over the partridge joints.

Cover and cook in the centre of the oven for about 1 hour, until the partridge joints are quite tender. *Serves 4–6.*

Stewed Venison

1 lb. meat from shoulder of venison,
  cut into ½-inch cubes
3 level tbsps. seasoned flour
1 oz. dripping or lard
2 onions, skinned and chopped

2 carrots, peeled and sliced
1 pint stock
Salt and pepper
Bouquet garni
2 tsps. vinegar

OVEN TEMPERATURE: 325°F (mark 3)

Toss the meat in the seasoned flour and fry it in the fat for 8–10 minutes, until well browned; remove from the pan, draining well, and put into a casserole. Fry the vegetables in the fat for about 5 minutes, until golden brown, remove from the pan, again draining well, and put into the casserole. Stir the rest of the seasoned flour into the fat remaining in the pan and cook slowly until brown. Remove the pan from the heat and gradually stir in the stock; return to the heat bring to the boil and continue stirring until it thickens. Pour the sauce over the venison, season, and add the bouquet garni and vinegar. Cover and cook in the centre of the oven for 2–2½ hours, until the meat is tender.

Remove the bouquet garni before serving the venison. *Serves 4.*

Pheasant with Chestnuts

1 pheasant, plucked, drawn, and
    jointed
1 tbsp. olive oil
1 oz. butter
½ lb. chestnuts, peeled
2 medium-sized onions, skinned and
    sliced
3 level tbsps. flour

¾ pint stock
1 wineglass Burgundy
Salt and pepper
Grated rind and juice of ½ orange
2 tsps. redcurrant jelly
Bouquet garni
Chopped parsley for garnish

OVEN TEMPERATURE: 350°F (mark 4)

Fry the pheasant in the oil and butter for about 5–6 minutes, until golden brown. Remove from the pan with a slotted spoon and put in a casserole. Fry the chestnuts and onions in the oil and butter for about 5 minutes, until golden brown, and add to the pheasant. Stir the flour into the remaining fat and cook for 2–3 minutes. Remove the pan from the heat and gradually add the stock and wine; return to the heat, bring to the boil and continue to stir until it thickens. Season, and pour over the pheasant. Add the orange rind and juice, redcurrant jelly, and bouquet garni, cover, and cook in the centre of the oven for 1 hour or until the pheasant is tender.

Remove the bouquet garni before serv- and adjust the seasoning, if necessary. Sprinkle with chopped parsley. *Serves 4.*

Casserole of Pheasant

1 pheasant, plucked and drawn
2 oz. butter
¼ lb. cooked ham, diced
Salt

¾ pint stock
¼ lb. button mushrooms, washed
4 tbsps. redcurrant jelly

OVEN TEMPERATURE: 350°F (mark 4)

Fry the bird on all sides in the melted butter until browned. Put in a casserole, add the ham, salt, and stock, and cook in the centre of the oven for 2 hours. Add the mushrooms after about 1½ hours and stir in the jelly just before serving. *Serves 4.*

CHAPTER 7
Top-of-the-Stove Casseroles

Here's a chapter, full of variety, that you'll find particularly useful if you have other plans for using your oven. All these delicious and exciting dishes are cooked on top of the stove. You'll discover that for all casserole cookery (but particularly this type) a really heavy, flameproof pan with a tight-fitting lid is invaluable: it'll prevent evaporation of the liquid and avoid the risk of sticking or burning. And of course if it's non-stick as well, so much the better!

Canard Montmorency

A 4–4½-lb. duckling, quartered
1 level tsp. salt
1 oz. butter
1 tbsp. corn oil
4 tbsps. Madeira
A 14-oz. can stoned black cherries, drained

3 level tsps. cornflour
2 tbsps. giblet stock
Salt and pepper
Watercress
Lattice potatoes

Sprinkle duckling joints with salt. Heat the butter and oil in a large saucepan and brown the joints on all sides. Remove from the pan, drain off fat, and wipe the pan clean. Replace duckling in pan in a single layer. Pour on the Madeira and the juice from cherries. Bring to the boil, cover, and simmer for about 40 minutes or until tender. Lift the joints from the pan, drain well, and keep warm on a serving dish.

Skim fat from pan juices. Blend cornflour with stock and stir into juices. Bring to the boil, add cherries, and heat through; check seasoning. Pour over the duckling. Garnish with watercress and lattice potatoes. *Serves 4.*

Austrian Veal and Vegetable Ragoût

¾ lb. veal
2 carrots, sliced
2 onions, skinned and sliced
2–3 sticks of celery, sliced
½ cauliflower, divided into sprigs
1¼ pints stock

4 oz. frozen peas
4 oz. mushrooms
1½ oz. butter
1½ oz. flour
Salt and pepper
A squeeze of lemon juice

Wash and trim the meat, cut into neat pieces, and put into a large saucepan with the fresh vegetables and stock. Simmer until meat is tender – 1¼–1½ hours. About 5 minutes before the cooking is completed add the peas. Fry the mushrooms in butter until tender, and mix with the other vegetables.

Make a roux with the butter and flour. Strain off the vegetable juices (keep the vegetables hot), gradually add to the roux, bring to the boil and allow to thicken, stir-

Canard Montmorency

Chicken Flamingo

ring all the time – 3–4 minutes. Put the meat and vegetables in a casserole. Add seasoning and lemon juice to sauce and pour onto the meat and vegetables. *Serves 4.*

Chicken Flamingo

4 oz. streaky bacon, rinded and diced
8 oz. long grain rice
1 pkt. onion sauce mix
1½ pints water

12 oz. cooked chicken, diced
2 large caps canned pimiento, sliced
Chopped parsley for garnish

Fry the bacon in its own fat till crisp. Stir in the rice till well coated in fat, then sauté for 3 minutes. Stir in the sauce mix, then add water. Bring to the boil, stirring, and simmer gently till all the liquid has been absorbed and the rice is tender. Stir fre- quently to prevent sticking. Add chicken and pimiento and heat through. Turn on to a hot serving dish and sprinkle with parsley. *Serves 4.*

A 2½-lb. cooked chicken yields approx. 12 oz. meat.

Poulet-Salami Basquais

2 oz. lard
4 large joints of chicken
1 onion, skinned and sliced
¼ level tsp. dried thyme
Bay leaf
Strip of orange rind
A 6-oz. piece salami

Salt and pepper
1 pint chicken stock
2 red peppers, seeded and sliced
½ lb. tomatoes, skinned and chopped
3 level tsps. paprika pepper
8 oz. long-grain rice

Melt 1 oz. lard in a large saucepan and brown the chicken well on all sides. Remove from pan. Add onion to pan and fry for a few minutes. Replace the chicken with

Poulet-Salami Basquais (*see page* 77)

thyme, bay leaf, orange rind, salami in one piece, salt, and pepper. Pour on the stock, cover, and simmer for about 40 minutes until chicken is tender. Strain off stock and discard thyme, bay leaf, and orange rind. Keep chicken and salami hot. Reduce stock to one-third. Melt remaining lard in a pan, add peppers, tomatoes, paprika, and reduced chicken stock. Boil, uncovered, until sauce is reduced to a coating consistency. Adjust seasoning.

Meanwhile, cook rice in boiling salted water until tender; drain. Arrange on a hot dish. Top with chicken and pour sauce over. Garnish with skinned and sliced cooked salami. *Serves 4.*

Caramelled Orange Chicken (*picture on front cover*)

A 3-lb. oven-ready chicken, jointed into 8
8 rashers streaky bacon (approx. 6 oz.), rinded
2 tbsps. oil
½ oz. butter
1 oz. caster sugar
1 tbsp. vinegar

¼ pint giblet stock
½ lb. firm tomatoes, blanched, skinned and sliced
Grated rind and juice of one small orange
Salt and freshly ground black pepper
Chopped parsley for garnish

Make a stock from the giblets. Wrap each chicken joint in a bacon rasher. (Stretch the bacon if necessary by drawing the blade of the knife along each rasher.)

Secure with a cocktail stick. Fry joints in the oil and butter in a shallow flameproof casserole (large enough to take joints in a single layer) for 5 minutes until golden brown. Drain the chicken and wipe the casserole clean with kitchen paper. Heat the sugar in the casserole until it turns golden, add the vinegar, giblet stock, tomatoes, and grated rind and orange juice. Season.

Replace joints, cover with a tightly fitting lid, and simmer on top of cooker for about $1\frac{1}{4}$ hours. Remove joints when cooked and reduce pan juices to a thick glaze. Replace chicken joints, spoon juices over chicken; sprinkle with parsley to garnish. *Serves 4.*

This dish can also be made with the chicken cut in half only, and cooked for about $2\frac{1}{2}$ hours.

Chicken Jambalaya

$\frac{1}{2}$ cooked chicken
2 onions, skinned and sliced
1 green pepper, seeded and chopped
2 sticks of celery, scrubbed and chopped
2 tbsps. oil
$\frac{1}{4}$ lb. mushrooms, washed and sliced

$\frac{3}{4}$ lb. tomatoes, skinned and quartered
$\frac{1}{4}$ pint chicken stock
$\frac{1}{4}$ pint dry white wine (optional)
6 oz. long-grain rice
$\frac{1}{4}$ lb. ham, chopped
Salt and pepper

Cut the chicken flesh into cubes. Sauté the onions, pepper, and celery in the oil until they are golden brown. Add the mushrooms, tomatoes, stock, wine, and rice and cook gently on top of the stove for 15–20 minutes, until the rice is tender. Add the chicken and ham and heat through. Season to taste. *Serves 4.*

Chicken Gumbo

1 onion, skinned and sliced
A small green pepper, thinly sliced
1 clove garlic, skinned and crushed
1 oz. butter
1 level tbsp. flour
An 8-oz. can tomatoes
A small can okra (ladies' fingers), drained
A $2\frac{1}{4}$-oz. can concentrated tomato purée
1 beef stock cube

2 tsps. Worcestershire sauce
Pinch of ground cloves
Pinch of chilli powder
Pinch of dried basil
$\frac{1}{2}$ bay leaf
Salt and pepper
$\frac{2}{3}$ pint water
12 oz. cooked chicken, diced
6 oz. long-grain rice, freshly cooked
Parsley, chopped

Sauté onion, pepper, and garlic in butter until soft. Blend in the flour and cook until bubbling. Add all the other ingredients except chicken, rice, and parsley. Simmer, covered, for 45 minutes, then add chicken and reheat. Toss the hot rice and parsley together. Put into individual dishes, hollow the centre, and spoon gumbo over. *Serves 4.*

Shrimp Chowder (*above*) and
Casseroled Beef (*below*)

Chicken Fricassee

A 1-lb. 12-oz. boned, rolled, and
  netted chicken
2 oz. butter
½ pint water
A pkt. onion sauce mix

¼ pint milk
2 tbsps. cream
Lemon juice
Chopped parsley and bacon rolls
  for garnish

Remove netting from bird and discard skin by unwrapping. Cut chicken flesh into neat pieces. Melt the butter in a flameproof casserole, sauté chicken until firm but not coloured. Add water, cover, and simmer for about 1 hour or until chicken is fork-tender. Do not season at this stage.

Blend sauce mix with milk, add chicken liquor, reduce to ¼ pint by rapid boiling. Return to chicken in casserole and cook gently for a further 15 minutes. Add cream and lemon to taste. Garnish chicken with parsley and bacon rolls. *Serves 4.*

Shrimp Chowder

2 onions, skinned and sliced
1½ oz. butter
5 medium potatoes, peeled and
  sliced
¼ pint boiling water
1 level tsp. salt

¼ level tsp. pepper
1 pint peeled shrimps or 1 8-oz.
  pkt. frozen shrimps
1½ pints milk
¼ lb. Cheddar cheese, grated
1 tbsp. chopped parsley

Fry the onions gently in the butter for 5 minutes, until soft. Add the potatoes, water, and seasoning, then cover and simmer for 15–20 minutes, or until potatoes are tender but not losing their shape. Add the shrimps,

milk, and cheese, and heat gently, stirring from time to time, until the cheese has melted. Pour the chowder into a deep bowl and sprinkle with the chopped parsley before serving. *Serves 4.*

Casseroled Beef

1½ lb. chuck steak or shin of beef
1 oz. flour
Salt and pepper
1 oz. dripping
2 onions, skinned and sliced

½ pint stock
½ lb. tomatoes, skinned
3–4 sticks of celery, scrubbed and
  chopped

Cut the meat into even-sized pieces and dip these in seasoned flour. Heat the dripping in a flameproof casserole and fry the sliced onions and meat until brown. Add the stock, tomatoes, and sliced celery. Cover,

and cook gently for about 2 hours.
  If desired, carrots, green peas, beans, cauliflower etc., may be added during the last ½ hour of cooking. *Serves 4–6.*

Beef Goulash

Beef Goulash

$1\frac{1}{2}$ lb. chuck or blade bone steak
2 oz. dripping or lard
1 lb. onions, skinned and thinly sliced
1 level tbsp. flour
$1\frac{1}{2}$ level tbsps. paprika
$\frac{1}{2}$ pint water

3 large tomatoes, skinned and chopped
Salt
1 lb. old potatoes, peeled
A 5-oz. carton plain yoghurt
Chopped parsley for garnish

Cut steak into 2-in. cubes and fry in a saucepan with dripping until sealed and brown. Put on one side. Fry onions until beginning to colour, then stir in the flour and paprika; cook for 3 minutes. Gradually stir in the water and bring to the boil. Add the tomato and meat, season with salt, and simmer, covered, until meat is nearly tender – about $1\frac{1}{2}$ hours. Stir occasionally during the cooking.

Add the potatoes cut in small cubes. Simmer for a further 1 hour. Spoon into a hot dish, and top with yoghurt and chopped parsley. *Serves 4.*

Somerset Honey Pork

$1\frac{1}{4}$ lb. lean pork
1 tbsp. oil
1 oz. butter
$\frac{1}{2}$ lb. cooking apples, peeled and diced

A 15-fl. oz. bottle cider
$\frac{1}{2}$ lemon
Sprig of thyme
Salt and pepper
1 tbsp. honey

Cut pork into even-sized ½-in. cubes, fry quickly in oil and butter in a shallow flame-proof casserole to seal. Remove, add the apples, toss until brown. Drain off fat, add the cider and, with a wooden spoon, stir the sediment on the base of the pan into the cider. Add the thinly-pared rind of half a lemon and a sprig of thyme, salt, and pepper. Cover with a tightly fitting lid and simmer very gently for about 1¼ hours.

Add one tbsp. lemon juice and the honey to the casserole and reduce liquid by half over a strong heat. *Serves 4.*

Bigos

¼ lb. leg or shoulder pork
Flour
¼ lb. cooked Polish ham
2 oz. flat mushrooms
1 lb. Polish sauerkraut, bottled or
  canned
Bay leaf
Water
1 lb. firm cabbage heart, shredded

¼ lb. streaky bacon rashers, rinded
1 large onion, skinned and chopped
2 oz. Polish sausage, skinned and
  diced
2 level tbsps. concentrated tomato
  paste
¼ pint dry red wine
1 clove garlic, skinned and crushed

Cut pork in 2-in. pieces, dredge with flour, cut ham and mushrooms into strips. Drain the sauerkraut, put into pan with the bay leaf and ½ pint water. Bring to boil, simmer for ½ hour. Meanwhile, put the cabbage and mushrooms into a second pan, add ½ pint water and cook in the same way. Cut bacon in pieces and fry; add to sauerkraut. Fry the onion until golden in the bacon fat; add to the sauerkraut. Add more fat if necessary, then fry pork until golden and add to the sauerkraut. Simmer for about 1 hour until pork is quite tender. After 30 minutes, add the cabbage, ham, sausage, tomato paste, wine, and garlic. Season to taste.

Bigos should be just juicy, not swimming in liquid. A little extra boiling water can be added during the cooking if necessary. Serve with rye bread or floury boiled potatoes. *Serves 4–6.*

Pork Chops in Orange-Pepper Sauce

4 trimmed loin chops
Salt and pepper
1 oz. sugar
1 oz. butter
1 clove garlic, peeled and sliced
1 oz. cornflour

½ level tsp. dried rosemary
½ pint water
3 tbsps. lemon juice
3 tbsps. orange juice
½ green pepper, chopped
6 thick slices fresh orange

Season both sides of chops with salt, pepper. and a little sugar. Melt butter in a frying pan and brown the chops well on both sides with the garlic. Place chops on one

Pork Chops in Orange-Pepper
Sauce (*see page* 83) and Danish
Pork Casserole (*below*)

side; discard garlic. Add the rest of the
sugar, cornflour, and rosemary to the drippings. Stir well and gradually add the
water. Cook, stirring until glossy. Add the
juices and green pepper. Return chops to
the pan and place a slice of orange on top
of each chop.

Cover with a lid, plate, or foil. Simmer
over a low heat for 40 minutes until chops
are tender. Uncover for the last 10 minutes. Baste occasionally. Serve garnished
with fresh half slices of orange. *Serves 4.*

Danish Pork Casserole

Salt and pepper
2 lb. pork fillet
¼ lb. butter
1 level tsp. sugar
12–15 button onions, skinned
**½ lb. tomatoes, skinned, quartered
  and seeded**
½ lb. button mushrooms
¼ pint single cream
½ lb. frozen peas, freshly-cooked
1 level tbsp. flour

Season the pork fillet and fry in 2 oz. butter
until evenly brown. Drain off the butter
into a small pan. Add ½ pint water to the
fillet, cover tightly, and simmer until
tender – about 1 hour.

Meanwhile, add the sugar to drained
butter and cook the onions until golden
and tender. Drain from pan, and cook the
tomatoes until well glazed. In a clean pan,
melt the remaining 2 oz. butter and sauté
the mushrooms for 1–2 minutes. Drain off
the juices, stir in the cream, and add onions,
tomatoes, and peas.

Remove the meat from the pan, cut into
serving pieces and turn into a shallow
casserole. Blend together the flour and ¼
pint water until smooth. Add to the meat

liquor, bring to the boil to thicken, and cook for a few minutes. Stir gravy into the vegetables, adjust seasoning and reheat. Pour over the pork. *Serves 6.*

Scalloped Gammon and Potatoes

2 thick gammon rashers (8 oz. each)
Water
1 oz. butter
¼ lb. mushrooms, stalked and sliced
Bay leaf
1 or 2 stalks of celery, scrubbed
1 lb. potatoes, peeled and thickly sliced
Parsley

Rind gammon rashers and snip the fat at intervals. In a shallow flameproof casserole, cover gammon with water, bring to the boil, and pour off the water. Put gammon on one side. Melt butter in the casserole, sauté mushrooms until just soft, drain, and put on one side. Return gammon to casserole, add bay leaf and celery cut in pieces. Pour over ½ pint water, cover, and simmer for ½ hour.

Discard bay leaf and celery. Lift gammon and place sliced potato underneath. Cook, covered, until potatoes are soft – the water should nearly be absorbed (about 25 minutes). Top each rasher with sautéd mushrooms and return to heat just to warm the mushrooms. Garnish with parsley. *Serves 2.*

Lamb and Dumpling Casserole

2 tbsps. oil
2 lb. scrag of lamb, cut into serving-size pieces
½ lb. carrots, peeled and cut into matchsticks
6 oz. onion, skinned and chopped
Bay leaf
4 cloves
¼ level tsp. dried thyme
1 level tbsp. concentrated tomato paste
1 golden Oxo cube
Salt and pepper

FOR DUMPLINGS:
8 oz. self-raising flour
½ level tsp. salt
3 oz. suet
Chopped parsley for garnish

Heat the oil in a large flameproof casserole, add the lamb, and fry until golden. Remove the meat, add the carrots and onions, cover, and cook for 10–15 minutes. Pour off the excess fat, return meat to the pan, add the herbs and seasonings, and pour over 1½ pints water. Bring to the boil, adjust seasoning, cover, and simmer for about 1¾ hours.

Meanwhile make up the flour, salt, suet, and a little water into 8 dumplings. Add to the casserole about ½ hour before the end of cooking time. Sprinkle liberally with chopped parsley before serving. *Serves 4.*

Lamb and Pasta Casserole

2 lb. scrag end of lamb
2 tbsps. cooking oil
1 large turnip, peeled and diced
3 leeks, sliced and washed
1 medium swede, peeled and sliced

$\frac{3}{4}$ pint stock or water
2 large carrots, peeled and grated
4 oz. medium pasta shapes
Salt and freshly ground pepper

Discard any surplus fat from the meat. Gently fry meat in oil to seal and colour the outer surface. In a large saucepan place meat, turnip, leeks, and swede. Pour in the stock and slowly bring to the boil, reduce heat, cover, and cook for about $1\frac{1}{4}$ hours. Add the grated carrot and pasta shapes and season to taste; continue to cook for a further 10 minutes. Adjust seasoning if necessary before serving. *Serves 4.*

Cutlet Stew

Cutlet Stew

8 lamb cutlets
Seasoned flour
Dripping
1 pint stock
Salt and freshly ground pepper

$\frac{3}{4}$ lb. carrots, scraped and quartered
12–15 button onions, skinned
2 green peppers, seeded and sliced
3 tomatoes, skinned and quartered

Trim cutlets and remove any surplus fat. Toss the cutlets in the seasoned flour and fry in the hot dripping until evenly browned on the outside. Remove from the pan, add any surplus flour, and make a gravy with the stock and seasonings. Return the meat to the pan with the carrots, onions, and peppers, bring to the boil, cover, and cook slowly for $1-1\frac{1}{4}$ hours.

About 20 minutes before the stew is ready, add the tomatoes. *Serves 4.*

CHAPTER 8
Made with Mince

If you've never cooked anything more exciting with mince than hamburgers or shepherd's pie, here is your chance to try something new. In this chapter we offer you a dozen recipes using mince in all sorts of mouthwatering ways that will give your family a real treat. When you're buying mince from the butcher do buy the best, it's well worth the extra few pence – and if you can persuade him to mince it for you from a piece of meat you've chosen yourself it's all to the good.

Sweet-sour Pork Balls

1 lb. pork, minced
1 clove garlic, skinned and crushed
1½ oz. flour
2 oz. fresh white breadcrumbs
Salt and pepper
1 egg yolk
1 oz. lard

SAUCE:
3 oz. sugar

4 tbsps. cider vinegar
3 tbsps. soy sauce
1½ level tbsps. cornflour
¼ pint water
1 green pepper, blanched and cut in
  thin strips
½ lb. tomatoes, skinned and
  quartered
An 11-oz. can crushed pineapple

Mix together the pork, garlic, ½ oz. flour, breadcrumbs, salt, and pepper. Add the egg yolk and mix well. Form into 24 balls and toss in the remaining 1 oz. flour. Heat lard in a frying pan. Add balls and fry gently for 20 minutes, turning frequently until golden brown.

Meanwhile, put sugar, vinegar, and soy sauce in a saucepan. Blend cornflour with the water and add to ingredients in pan. Bring to the boil, stirring. Simmer gently for 5 minutes then add green pepper, tomatoes, and pineapple. Simmer for a further 5 minutes. To serve, put pork balls into a warmed casserole and pour the sauce over. *Serves 4.*

Moussaka

3 aubergines (1½ lb. approx.)
Flour
4 tbsps. oil
4 medium-sized onions, skinned and
  thinly sliced
1 lb. lean beef or lamb, minced
4 firm tomatoes, skinned and thickly
  sliced

¼ pint well-seasoned stock
¼ pint thick tomato purée
2 large eggs
¼ pint single cream
Salt and freshly ground pepper

OVEN TEMPERATURE: 350°F (mark 4)

Sweet-sour Pork Balls

Slice aubergines and dust with flour. Fry in 2 tbsps oil. When beginning to colour, drain, and arrange round a shallow 4½-pint casserole. Add 1 tbsp. oil to the pan and when reheated fry onions and meat until lightly browned. Place on top of aubergines. Fry tomatoes in 1 tbsp. oil and add to the dish. Pour in the stock and the tomato purée. Bake, uncovered, in the oven for about 45 minutes.

Beat together the eggs and cream, season well, and pour over the contents of the casserole. Return to the oven and continue to cook for a further 15–20 minutes until sauce is set and golden. *Serves 4–6.*

Mince and Tomato Cobbler

1 lb. lean beef, minced
6 oz. onion, peeled and chopped
An 8-oz. can whole tomatoes
1 tbsp. Worcestershire sauce
Salt and freshly ground black pepper
2 oz. butter or margarine

8 oz. self-raising flour
1 level tsp. baking powder
2 eggs, beaten
¼ pint milk
2 oz. Cheddar cheese, grated
Chopped parsley for garnish

OVEN TEMPERATURE: 400°F (mark 6)

Cook the mince in a thick-based frying-pan until the fat begins to run. Add the onion and cook until tender. Pour off excess fat, add the tomatoes and Worcestershire sauce and bubble until no juice remains. Season well. Rub fat into sifted flour, baking powder, and ½ level tsp. salt. Mix into a fairly stiff dough with cold water. Roll out and stamp into 2-in. rounds. Line the sides of a 2½-pint shallow ovenproof dish with the scones, stood on end. Spoon in the meat. Whisk eggs and milk, add ½ level tsp. salt and ground pepper, and pour over mince. Top with grated cheese and bake for about 40 minutes.

Serve sprinkled with chopped parsley. *Serves 4.*

Chilli Con Carne (1)

12 oz. haricot or butter beans
Pinch bicarbonate of soda
1½ lb. beef, minced
½ oz. fat or oil
1 large onion, skinned and chopped
1 green pepper, seeded and chopped
(optional)

A 15-oz. can tomatoes
Salt and pepper
1–2 level tsps. chilli powder
1 tbsp. vinegar
1 level tsp. sugar

OVEN TEMPERATURE: 325°F (mark 3)

Soak the beans overnight in cold water with the bicarbonate of soda. Fry the beef in the fat or oil until lightly browned, then add the onion and pepper and fry for a further 5 minutes until soft. Stir in the beans and tomatoes and add seasoning and chilli powder blended with the vinegar and sugar. Cover, and simmer on top of the stove or in the oven for 2–2½ hours, until tender. *Serves 4.*

Chilli Con Carne (2)

1 lb. beef, minced
A 10-oz. can red kidney beans

8 level tbsps. tomato/chilli chutney
½ tsp. Tabasco sauce

Slowly fry the minced beef without additional fat. When browned, add the juice from the kidney beans, reserving the beans for use later. Stir in the chutney and Tabasco sauce. Mix together well. Cover the pan and cook over a *low* heat for 1–1¼

hours. Stir occasionally, adding ¼ pint water at about half-time. The mince should be creamy.

Fold through the whole beans and reheat. Serve in small bowls with a crisp green salad. *Serves 4.*

Stuffed Marrow (1)

A 3-lb. marrow
1 tbsp. oil
2 medium onions, peeled and chopped
8 oz. lean beef, minced
4 tomatoes, skinned, seeded, and diced

1 tbsp. chopped parsley
1½ oz. breadcrumbs
1½ oz. Cheddar cheese, grated
Salt and pepper

OVEN TEMPERATURE: 375°F (mark 5)

Slice the end off the marrow, reserve, and scoop out the seeds with the handle of a spoon. Blanch the marrow in a pan of boiling salted water for 5 minutes; drain. Heat oil and fry onion until golden and soft. Add meat to pan and fry slowly until coloured – about 15 minutes. Remove from the heat and add the tomatoes, parsley, bread-

crumbs and cheese. Season well. Fill the marrow cavity with the beef stuffing, replace the end, and secure with cocktail sticks. Place in a roasting pan, cover with greased foil, and cook in the oven for 45–60 minutes.

Serve with a rich gravy or tomato sauce. *Serves 4–6.*

Cottage Pie

1 lb. beef, minced
½ oz. butter
1 pkt. onion sauce mix
¼ pint water

2 canned pimiento, chopped
½ lb. tomatoes, skinned and chopped
2 lbs. potatoes, boiled and creamed
Salt and pepper

OVEN TEMPERATURE: 425°F (mark 7)

Melt the butter in a saucepan and add the mince. Cook, stirring, for about 10 minutes. Sprinkle over the onion sauce mix and add the water, pimiento, and tomatoes. Stir well and cook for a further 10 minutes.

Adjust seasoning and turn into an ovenproof dish. Top with the creamed potato, fork over the surface. Place dish on a baking sheet and cook for about ½ hour or until potato is deep golden brown. *Serves 4.*

Beef Balls en Casserole

Beef Balls en Casserole

4 tbsps. corn oil
1 large onion, skinned and sliced
1 clove of garlic, crushed
1 lb. lean beef, minced
2 oz. fresh white breadcrumbs
2 tsps. Worcestershire sauce
Salt and pepper
1 egg, beaten

1 oz. flour
1 lb. carrots, peeled and sliced
1 lb. potatoes, peeled
A 15-oz. can tomatoes
½ level tsp. dried sage
Bay leaf
1 pint beef stock (using stock cube)
Parsley for garnish (optional)

OVEN TEMPERATURE: 350°F (mark 4)

Heat 2 tbsps. of oil in a frying-pan, add onion, and fry until light golden brown. Add garlic. Drain and place in a 4½-pint casserole. Meanwhile mix together minced beef, breadcrumbs, Worcestershire sauce, salt, pepper, and egg. Work together, then form into 16 balls. Toss balls in flour. Heat remaining oil in frying-pan, and fry meat balls until light golden brown (about 10 minutes). Add to casserole with carrots.

Cut potatoes into 1-in. cubes and add to casserole with tomatoes, sage, bay leaf, and stock. Season, cover, and cook in centre of oven for 1½ hours. Serve sprinkled with chopped parsley. *Serves 4.*

Meatballs in Mushroom Sauce

1 lb. beef, minced
Salt and pepper
A good dash of Worcestershire sauce
1 level tsp. mixed herbs
1 medium onion, finely chopped
1 clove garlic, crushed

1 egg, beaten
Flour
2 tbsps. corn oil
1 pkt. mushroom sauce mix
Button mushrooms and parsley for
   garnish

OVEN TEMPERATURE: 350°F (mark 4)

Mix together the mince, seasonings, Worcestershire sauce, herbs, onion, and garlic, then bind with egg. Divide into 8 and roll into balls, using a little flour. Fry in the oil until browned, drain, and transfer to a casserole. Make sauce according to directions on the packet, using ½ pint milk. Pour over meat balls, cover, and cook for about 45 minutes. Garnish with sautéd mushrooms and parsley. *Serves 4.*

Meatballs in Mushroom Sauce

Spicy Meatballs

1 lb. beef, minced
4 oz. fresh breadcrumbs
1 egg, beaten
⅛ pint milk
Salt and pepper
½ level tsp. thyme
1 tbsp. oil
1 onion, skinned and chopped

1 clove garlic, skinned and crushed
1 level tbsp. flour
A 15-oz. can tomatoes
¼ pint stock
1 level tsp. concentrated tomato
  paste
Chopped parsley for garnish

OVEN TEMPERATURE: 350°F (mark 4)

In a mixing bowl, mix together the meat, breadcrumbs, egg, milk, and seasonings. Form the mixture into ¾-inch balls and fry in the oil until brown. Remove from the pan and place in a casserole dish. Fry the onion and garlic until soft and add the flour, mix well and stir in the tomatoes, stock, and paste. Cook until thick and adjust seasoning. Pour the sauce over the meatballs and cover the casserole. Cook for 45 minutes.

Serve hot, garnished with chopped parsley and accompanied by rice. *Serves 6.*

Lasagne

2 14-oz. cans tomatoes, drained
1 level tbsp. concentrated tomato
  paste
1 level tsp. dried marjoram
Salt and freshly milled pepper
1 lb. beef, minced
4 oz. lasagne

1 oz. butter
1 oz. flour
½ pint milk
3 oz. Cheddar cheese, grated
Oil for glazing
8 oz. Mozzarella cheese, sliced

OVEN TEMPERATURE: 375°F (mark 5)

Combine the canned tomatoes, tomato paste, marjoram, salt, and pepper. Simmer in an open pan for 30 minutes. Add the mince and simmer for a further 25 minutes to reduce. Cook the lasagne for 10–15 minutes in a large pan of fast-boiling salted water; drain. In a small saucepan melt the butter, stir in flour, and gradually add the milk. Bring to the boil, stirring constantly. Remove from heat, add cheese, and season. Cover the base of a 9-in. fluted flan case with strips of lasagne. Add alternate layers of meat and cheese sauce. Finish final layer with strips of lasagne placed diagonally across, with the sauces between. Lightly oil lasagne to prevent drying.

Bake for about 30 minutes. Remove from the oven, add the Mozzarella between lasagne strips and return to the oven at 425°F (mark 7) until golden and bubbling. *Serves 4.*

Pot Luck Pie

2 lb. old potatoes, peeled
1 lb. cooked beef or lamb
½ lb. each of onions and carrots,
  peeled
1 beef stock cube (dissolved in ½ pint
  water)

1 level tbsp. cornflour
1 tsp. Worcestershire sauce
Salt and pepper
Chopped parsley for garnish

OVEN TEMPERATURE: 400°F (mark 6)

Cook potatoes and mash with butter. Meanwhile mince together the beef, onions, and carrots and put into a saucepan with the stock. Blend cornflour with 2 tbsps. water. Add to the meat, bring to the boil, stirring, and simmer for 5 minutes. Add Worcestershire sauce and season to taste. Turn into an ovenproof dish, fork or pipe potato on top, and cook for 30 minutes or until golden brown.

Sprinkle generously with chopped parsley. *Serves 4–6.*

CHAPTER 9
Oven-cooked Vegetables

Casseroled vegetables? Yes – it's a really different way of cooking an essential part of the meal. Particularly useful if there's a glut of a certain vegetable and the family are tired of having it served your usual way! You can cook the vegetables in the oven at the same time as a meat or fish stew, or try one of the mixed vegetable casseroles with pasta or cheese – you'll find it tasty, filling, and economical.

Ratatouille

½ lb. courgettes, trimmed
½ lb. aubergine, trimmed
Salt
10 tbsps. olive oil
½ lb. onions, skinned and thinly sliced

2 green peppers, seeded and sliced
2 cloves garlic, skinned and crushed
Ground black pepper
1 lb. firm ripe tomatoes, skinned
3 level tbsps. chopped parsley

OVEN TEMPERATURE: 325°F (mark 3)

Cut courgettes and aubergine into ¼-in. slices. Sprinkle vegetables with salt, leave to stand for ½–2 hours. Dry on absorbent paper. Heat 4 tbsps. olive oil in a large, thick-based frying-pan, add half the courgettes and aubergine in a single layer, and sauté on both sides until golden. Remove from the pan and cook remaining aubergine and courgettes in a further 4 tbsps. oil. Cook onions and peppers in a further 2 tbsps. oil for about 10 minutes. Stir in garlic and seasoning. Quarter tomatoes, add to onions and pepper, season further. Cook, covered, over a low heat for 5 minutes.

Place a third of the tomato mixture in a flameproof casserole, sprinkle over 1 tbsp. parsley. Arrange half the aubergine and courgettes on top, then half the remaining tomatoes and parsley. Finish with remaining aubergine, courgettes, tomatoes, and parsley. Cover and bake for about 1 hour. *Serves 6.*

Aubergine au Gratin

4 aubergines, sliced
Salt
8 rashers streaky bacon
2–3 tbsps. cooking oil
Freshly ground pepper
3 oz. parmesan cheese, grated

¼ pint single cream
¾ lb. firm tomatoes, skinned, seeded, and sliced
Fresh breadcrumbs
Butter

OVEN TEMPERATURE: 375°F (mark 5)

Wipe aubergines and cut in ¼-in. slices. Sprinkle with salt and leave to stand for 1 hour. Drain off liquid and pat dry with absorbent kitchen paper. Rind bacon, fry until crisp, then cut into small pieces with scissors. Heat oil in a large frying-pan and fry aubergine slices a few at a time until tinged with brown on both sides. Butter an ovenproof dish, place half the aubergines in the base. Season with pepper, sprinkle with a third of the cheese and pour over half the cream. Layer half the tomatoes and bacon. Repeat with the rest of the ingredients, finishing with the cheese. Lightly sprinkle with breadcrumbs and dot with butter.

Cook, uncovered, in the oven for about 45 minutes. Serve at once. *Serves 4.*

Cheese Potato Casserole

1½ lb. potatoes
½ lb. tomatoes
2 green peppers (optional)
1 onion, skinned
A little flour

6 oz. cheese, grated
Parsley, chopped
Salt and pepper
½ pint milk

OVEN TEMPERATURE: 400°F (mark 6)

Peel the potatoes and tomatoes, remove the seeds from the peppers (if used), and slice all the vegetables. Mix the flour, two-thirds of the cheese, parsley, salt, and pepper. Put layers of vegetables into a buttered casserole, sprinkling each layer with cheese mixture; finish with potato and a generous sprinkling of plain cheese. Pour in the milk and add water until the liquid comes about half-way up the casserole. Cover, and bake in the oven for about ¾ hour.

When the potatoes are nearly cooked, remove lid to brown top. *Serves 4.*

Cheese Scalloped Potatoes

1¼ lb. potatoes, peeled and sliced
6 oz. onion, peeled and sliced

1 pkt. cheese sauce mix
½ pint milk

OVEN TEMPERATURE: 375°F (mark 5)

Layer the potatoes and onions in a shallow ovenproof dish. Make up the sauce according to directions on the packet, using the milk. Pour over the potatoes, cover, and bake for 1¼–1½ hours. *Serves 4–5.*

Glazed Onions

4 oz. streaky bacon, rinded and
   diced
8 medium onions, skinned

½ pint stock
Water
1 pkt. parsley sauce mix

OVEN TEMPERATURE: 350°F (mark 4)

Fry bacon in its own fat and drain. Transfer to casserole with whole onions. Pour boiling stock over and bake for about $1\frac{1}{4}$ hours until onions are tender.

Strain off liquor, make up to $\frac{1}{2}$ pint with water, and use (instead of milk) to make up a sauce according to directions on the packet. Pour over onions and serve. *Serves 4.*

Baked Onions in Cider

1 lb. onions
1 oz. butter
1 level tsp. sugar

$\frac{1}{4}$ pint cider
Salt and freshly ground pepper

OVEN TEMPERATURE: 350°F (mark 4)

Peel and thickly slice the onions. Place in a small casserole and dab the butter over. Add the remaining ingredients, cover tightly, and cook in the oven for about $1\frac{1}{2}$ hours. Open the lid for the last 15 minutes. *Serves 4.*

Mushroom Casserole

$\frac{3}{4}$ lb. mushrooms
3 tomatoes
1 onion, skinned
1 oz. butter or dripping

1 sheep's kidney (optional)
Salt and pepper
1 tbsp. chopped parsley
4 tbsps. stock or water

OVEN TEMPERATURE: 350°F (mark 4)

Grease a casserole. Wash and slice the mushrooms, skin and slice the tomatoes; cut the onion in rings and fry in the fat until golden brown. Cut up the kidney. Fill the dish with alternate layers of kidney and vegetables, seasoning well. Sprinkle with the parsley and finish with a layer of mushrooms. Add the liquid and stew gently in the oven until tender – about 30 minutes. Pack the ingredients closely to allow for shrinkage during cooking. *Serves 3.*

Braised Celery

2 oz. butter
4 celery hearts, washed

Lemon juice
$\frac{1}{2}$ pint stock

OVEN TEMPERATURE: 325°F (mark 3)

Grease a shallow casserole with the butter, trim the celery hearts, and place in the casserole. Add a dash of lemon juice and the stock, cover with greased paper and the lid, and cook in the oven until the celery is tender – about 1 hour. Place it on a hot serving dish.

If necessary, reduce the liquor by boiling, then pour it over the celery. *Serves 4.*

Stuffed Marrow (2)

1 marrow (2 lb. approx.)
1 oz. butter
2 oz. cooked long-grain rice
8 oz. Cheddar cheese, grated
1 oz. salted peanuts, chopped

2 tomatoes, skinned, seeded, and
   chopped
Salt and pepper
2 eggs, beaten
8 rashers streaky bacon

OVEN TEMPERATURE: 350°F (mark 4)

Wipe marrow and peel. Cut off 4 in. from the end and scoop out the seeds with a spoon, or cut in half lengthwise and remove seeds. Melt butter and fry rice until light golden brown. Put the grated cheese, peanuts, tomatoes, salt, and pepper in a mixing bowl and bind together with the beaten eggs. Stuff the marrow, securing the top with cocktail sticks. Wrap the rashers of bacon around the marrow. Wrap in buttered foil, place on a baking tray or gratin dish, and bake in the oven for about 1¼ hours. Roll back the foil and cook for a further 15 minutes. *Serves 4.*

Braised Chicory

1½ lb. chicory, washed
1 oz. butter
¼ level tsp. grated nutmeg
Juice of ½ lemon
¼ pint chicken stock

1½ level tsps. cornflour
1 tbsp. cold water
2 tbsps. cream
Salt and freshly ground black pepper
Chopped parsley for garnish

OVEN TEMPERATURE: 325°F (mark 3)

Blanch the whole chicory heads in boiling, salted water for 5 minutes. Drain well. Butter a casserole large enough to take chicory in a single layer. Lay chicory in the base, dot with butter. Stir the nutmeg and lemon juice into the stock, pour over the chicory. Cover with buttered foil or a lid and cook in the oven for about 1½ hours. Blend the cornflour with the water. Drain the juices from the casserole into a small saucepan, add the cornflour, and bring to the boil, stirring; bubble for 1 minute. Add the cream but do not boil. Adjust seasoning. Pour over the chicory. Sprinkle with chopped parsley. *Serves 4.*

Vegetable Macaroni Casserole

½ lb. carrots, peeled
A small turnip, peeled
2 stalks celery, scrubbed
2 leeks, scrubbed
2 tomatoes, skinned
1 rasher bacon
1 oz. dripping

1 clove garlic, skinned and crushed
Salt and pepper
¼ pint tomato juice
2 oz. macaroni
4 tbsps. chopped parsley
Fried onion rings to garnish
Grated cheese as accompaniment

OVEN TEMPERATURE: 350°F (mark 4)

Cut up the vegetables and dice the bacon. Heat the fat and sauté first the bacon then the vegetables for 10 minutes. Transfer to a casserole, add the crushed garlic, seasoning, and tomato juice, and cook in a moderate oven for 1 hour.

Meanwhile cook the macaroni in boiling salted water; add with the parsley to the casserole and top with fried onion. Serve with cheese. *Serves 2.*

Boston Baked Beans

8–12 oz. haricot beans
½ lb. fat salt belly of pork
2 medium-sized onions, skinned and
  sliced
1½ level tsps. dry mustard
1–2 level tsps. salt

Freshly ground pepper
1 level tbsp. brown sugar
2 tbsps. black treacle
1–2 tbsps. cider vinegar
Pinch of ground cinnamon
Pinch of ground cloves

OVEN TEMPERATURE: 300°F (mark 2)

Wash the beans, cover with cold water, and leave to soak overnight. Drain, saving the water in which beans have been soaked. Cut pork into 1-in. cubes. Put the beans, onions, and pork into a large casserole, pour in just enough water to cover the beans, and stir in the remaining ingredients. Cover closely and cook in the oven for 8–9 hours. Stir occasionally, adding more water if the beans dry out while cooking. *Serves 4.*

CHAPTER 10
Curry Meals

Curries undoubtedly improve with long, slow cooking – a method which gives the flavours a real chance to develop. So the longer you can let the sauce cook, the better. You'll find here a wide selection of curries to choose from – mild or hot, using cooked or uncooked meat, fish, eggs, and vegetables. If you have a freezer, it's a good idea to make up double the quantity of sauce you'll be using and then freeze half of it for another time. We've also included in this chapter a variety of sambols, which traditionally accompany a curry meal.

Bindaloo Curry

1 lb. stewing steak
4 oz. butter
6 medium-sized onions, sliced
2 tbsps. curry powder

$\frac{1}{4}$ pint vinegar
Pinch of salt
Gherkins and olives, sliced

OVEN TEMPERATURE: 300°F (mark 2)

Cut up the steak, removing excess fat. Heat 2 oz. butter in a saucepan and brown the onions for 5 minutes with the lid on. Add curry powder and fry for a further 5 minutes. Brown the steak slightly in the remaining 2 oz. butter, then add it. Gradually add the vinegar and salt and simmer for 2 hours, or cook in the oven in a casserole. Garnish with gherkins and olives. *Serves 4.*

Madras Curry (Hot)

2 oz. almonds, chopped
2 oz. butter or fat
2 onions, chopped
1 clove garlic, chopped finely
1 tsp. coriander powder
1 tsp. black pepper
$\frac{1}{2}$ tsp. chilli powder
$\frac{1}{4}$ tsp. cardamom powder
$\frac{1}{2}$ tsp. cumin powder

Small piece of cinnamon stick
$\frac{1}{2}$ tsp. ground cloves
2 tsps. flour
1 pint stock or water
1 lb. meat (cut small)
2 tsps. turmeric powder
1 tsp. sugar
Salt
Juice of 1 lemon

Cover the almonds with $\frac{1}{4}$ pint boiling water and leave for 15 minutes, then strain the infusion. Melt the fat and lightly fry the onions and garlic. Add spices and flavourings (except turmeric), with the flour, cook for 5 minutes, then add the stock and meat. Simmer till tender – $1\frac{1}{2}$–2 hours. Add almond infusion, turmeric, sugar, and salt, and simmer for $\frac{1}{4}$ hour; finally, add lemon juice. *Serves 4.*

Bengal Curry

4 oz. butter
2 onions, thinly sliced
1 clove garlic, skinned and crushed
2 tbsps. curry powder
2 tsps. mixed spice
A good pinch of saffron

1 tbsp. lemon juice
1–1½ lb. tender meat or parboiled
   chicken, diced
1 tsp. salt
¾ pint stock

Heat the butter and fry the onions and crushed garlic until well browned, then add the curry powder, spice, saffron, and lemon juice, and fry again for 5–10 minutes. Add the meat, salt, and stock, and cook, stirring occasionally, for about ½ hour, by which time the stock should be partly absorbed and the curry thickened. Serve with pellao and a sambol. *Serves 4–6.*

Bengal Curry

Curried Chicken

4 large wing or leg chicken portions
3 tbsps. corn oil
1 pkt. onion sauce mix
½ pint milk
1 level tbsp. curry powder
1 tbsp. lemon juice

An 8-oz. can tomatoes
2 oz. sultanas
1 eating apple, peeled, cored, and
chopped
1 oz. shelled and blanched almonds
8 oz. long grain rice

OVEN TEMPERATURE: 350°F (mark 4)

Cut each piece of chicken into two. Fry the chicken in 2 tbsps. oil till beginning to brown. Drain, and place in a casserole. Make up sauce with the milk, according to directions on the packet. Stir in curry powder, lemon juice, and tomatoes, simmer for 2 minutes. Add sultanas and apple.

Pour over chicken, cover, and cook in the oven for 1½ hours.

In a small pan, heat 1 tbsp. oil and fry the almonds till golden. Drain and add to the chicken. Serve with freshly boiled rice. *Serves 4.*

Chicken and Banana Curry

A 4-lb. oven-ready chicken
Giblets
1 tbsp. corn oil
1½ oz. butter
1 lb. firm bananas
½ lb. onions, peeled and thinly sliced
4 oz. lean bacon, rinded and diced

2 level tsps. curry powder
1 oz. flour
2 level tsps. concentrated tomato
paste
4 tbsps. single cream
Salt and freshly ground black pepper

OVEN TEMPERATURE: 325°F (mark 3)

Joint the chicken into 12 pieces, discarding skin. In a small pan, cover the giblets with cold water, bring to the boil, and simmer for about ½ hour. Heat the oil in a thick-based pan, add 1 oz. butter and, on the point of browning, add the chicken pieces, flesh-side down. Fry for about 10 minutes until golden. Remove the chicken and place flesh-side uppermost in a casserole. Add a further ½ oz. butter to the pan, peel and thickly slice the banana, add to pan,

fry briefly until golden. Drain and add to the chicken. Fry the onion and bacon until tender in reheated pan juices. Stir in curry powder and flour. cook for 1 minute. Strain off the giblet stock. Pour over the onion and bring to the boil. Stir in the tomato paste and cream. Season well.

Pour sauce over the chicken. Cover, and cook in the oven for about 1¼ hours or until tender. *Serves 6.*

Ceylon Prawn Curry

1 onion, skinned and finely chopped
1 clove garlic, skinned and crushed
2 oz. butter
1 tbsp. flour
2 tsps. turmeric
1 tsp. ground cloves
1 tsp. ground cinnamon

1 tsp. salt
1 tsp. sugar
¼ pint coconut milk
½ pint stock
1 pint prawns or 1 doz. Dublin Bay
  prawns, shelled
1 tsp. lemon juice

Melt the butter in a pan and fry the onion and garlic lightly, then add the flour, turmeric, cloves, cinnamon, salt, and sugar. Cook gently for 10 minutes and add the coconut milk and stock. Simmer gently for a further 10 minutes, add the cooked prawns and lemon juice, re-season as necessary, and cook for a further 10 minutes.

Garnish with a few prawns heated separately; serve this mild curry with boiled rice and a hot chutney. *Serves 2.*

Shrimps may be used in a similar way.

Fish Curry

1 lb. filleted fish (e.g. cod or halibut)
2 small onions, skinned and sliced
A little garlic
2 oz. butter

1 tomato, skinned and quartered
2 tsps. curry powder
Salt to taste

Prepare the fish in the usual way. Fry the slices of onion and garlic in the fat, then add the tomato and 1 tbsp. water to make a thick paste. Sprinkle fish with curry powder and salt, add to the pan, and cook until golden brown. Pour in 1 teacupful warm water and let the curry cook in the pan with the lid on till the fish is tender when tested; take care not to let it break up. Serve with rice or puris. *Serves 4.*

Lemon juice may be included if desired, and the tomato replaced by tomato paste and a little extra stock or water.

Curried Kidney

½ lb. ox kidney
Seasoned flour
1 small onion, skinned
1 oz. dripping
2 tsps. curry powder
1 apple, peeled and chopped
1 tomato, skinned and sliced

1 tsp. curry paste
½ pint stock
1 tsp. lemon juice
2 tsps. chutney
Boiled rice
Parsley to garnish

Ceylon Prawn Curry

Soak the kidney in warm water, cut into small pieces, discarding the core, and toss in seasoned flour. Chop the onion finely and fry in the dripping until golden brown. Add the kidney and curry powder and fry for a few moments. Stir in the chopped apple, sliced tomato, and curry paste, then add the stock and bring to the boil, stirring continuously. Add the lemon juice and chutney and simmer gently for about 2 hours, until tender, taking care that the sauce does not stick or burn.

Cook the rice in the usual way. Dish up the kidney with a border of rice and sprinkled with parsley. *Serves 2.*

Curried Eggs

5 eggs, hardboiled
2 oz. butter
2 small onions, skinned and chopped
A small piece of apple, chopped
1 tsp. curry powder
1 oz. flour

½ pint stock
Salt
2 tsps. lemon juice
Boiled rice
Stuffed olives

Slice 3 of the eggs. Melt the butter, fry onion lightly, add the apple, curry powder, and flour, and cook for a few minutes. Gradually add the stock, salt, and lemon juice, boil up and skim, then simmer for about ¼ hour. Heat the sliced eggs in this sauce, then turn the mixture into a hot dish and surround with boiled rice.

Decorate with olives and remaining eggs, cut in wedges. Serve this mild curry with lemon, preserved ginger, and coconut. *Serves 3.*

Curried Veal

1 lb. lean veal
1 tbsp. curry powder
1 oz. seasoned flour
2 oz. butter
2 onions, skinned and sliced
1 pint white stock or water
2 tsps. curry paste

A little lemon juice
2 tbsps. single cream
A few pickled gherkins
1 tbsp. chutney
Chopped parsley and paprika pepper
  to garnish

Cut the meat into small pieces. Mix the curry powder and seasoned flour and use to coat the meat. Melt the butter in a saucepan and sauté the onions for a few minutes; remove the onions and fry the meat to a light brown. Add the stock and bring to the boil, stirring all the time. Return the onions to the pan, together with the curry paste; cover, and simmer gently until tender – about 1 hour. Shortly before serving, stir in

Curried Eggs

the lemon juice, cream, some chopped gherkins, and the chutney, with extra seasoning if necessary.

Arrange on a hot dish with a border of boiled rice and garnish with gherkin fans, chopped parsley, and paprika pepper. *Serves 4.*

Dry Veal Curry

1 lb. lean veal
2 medium-sized onions, skinned
1 clove garlic, skinned
1 oz. butter
2 tsps. curry powder
1 tsp. curry paste

Salt to taste
A few pickled gherkins
2 tsps. chutney
Juice of $\frac{1}{2}$ lemon
$\frac{1}{4}$ pint stock

Cut the meat up small. Chop the onions and garlic very finely and fry lightly in the butter. Add curry powder and paste and cook thoroughly for about 5 minutes, stirring all the time. Add the meat and salt and cook until well browned. Finally, add gherkins, chutney, lemon juice, and stock, and cook very slowly for $2-2\frac{1}{2}$ hours, stirring occasionally.

Serve with rice and lemon. *Serves 4.*

Dry Beef Curry

1 lb. stewing steak
1 tbsp. coriander powder
1 tsp. turmeric powder
Bay leaf
2 cloves
¼ tsp. chilli powder
½ tsp. cumin powder
A pinch of ground cinnamon

Tamarind water or diluted vinegar
2 oz. butter
1 onion, finely chopped
1 clove garlic, skinned and crushed
1 tsp. curry paste
½ pint stock or water
Salt to taste

Cut up the meat. Mix the spices and tamarind water to form a paste. Melt the butter and fry the onion and garlic, then fry the spices and curry paste thoroughly, stirring constantly. Add the meat and cook slowly for about 1 hour, stirring occasionally. Add the stock, cover, and cook gently for another hour, till liquid is absorbed. Adjust the seasoning, if necessary.

Serve with rice and chutney. *Serves 4.*

Curried Vegetables

½ turnip, peeled
½ lb. carrots, peeled
2 parsnips, peeled
2 medium-sized onions, skinned
3 tomatoes, skinned
¼ lb. butter beans, soaked

1 oz. dripping
2 tbsps. curry powder
2 tbsps. chutney
Salt and pepper
¼–½ pint stock

Prepare the vegetables and cut in small pieces; drain the beans. Melt the fat in a pan, add curry powder and cook over low heat for 5 minutes. Add the chutney, vegetables, and seasoning, then gradually add sufficient stock to make a sauce. Cook very gently till vegetables are tender – about 1½ hours.

Thicken with flour, if required, and serve with rice and lemon. *Serves 4.*

Biryani

A 4½-lb. leg of lamb, boned
A 5-fl. oz. carton natural yoghurt
1 level tbsp. curry powder
1 level tsp. curry paste
1 level tsp. chilli powder
1 lb. onions, skinned and sliced
3 oz. butter

1 lb. potatoes, peeled and diced
½ lb. long grain rice
¼ pint milk
A small sachet of powdered saffron
Garnish:
    4 oz. plump sultanas
    2 oz. flaked almonds, fried

OVEN TEMPERATURE: 325°F (mark 3)

Make about 1 pint of stock with the lamb bones. Cut the meat into 1-in. chunks, marinade for about 1 hour in the yoghurt, curry powder, paste, and chilli powder. Fry the onions in 1 oz. butter until golden. Remove, add the remaining butter, and, when beginning to brown, add the meat. Brown quickly over a fierce heat and remove. Put the stock in the pan, loosen any sediment, and add the potato, simmering for 10 minutes. Rain rice into a pan of boiling, salted water, return to the boil and cook for 10 minutes; at the same time infuse the saffron in the warmed milk. Drain the rice.

Place the lamb in a large (8-pint) shallow casserole. Combine the stock, potatoes, rice, saffron milk, 2 oz. sultanas, and onion. Season and place on top of the lamb. Top the casserole with foil and cover with a lid. Cook in the oven for about 1 hour. Garnish. *Serves 8.*

Pellao

2 onions, skinned
2 oz. butter
1 lb. rice
Chicken stock
Salt to taste

A few cloves
A little ground cardamom
A few pieces of stick cinnamon
A few peppercorns
A few sultanas

OVEN TEMPERATURE: 350°F (mark 4)

Mince 1 onion, fry it in the hot butter until pale golden brown, then add the uncooked rice and fry for about 5–6 minutes. Now add some stock, salt, and the spices, adding more stock as the rice swells. When the rice is well cooked, put the pellao in the oven for ½ hour to dry it off (or it may be dried by placing it in a saucepan over a very gentle heat. But Indian cooks generally find the oven more satisfactory). Slice the other onion, fry it with a few sultanas until golden brown and crisp, and sprinkle over the rice. *Serves 8.*

Yoghurt and Cucumber

½ cucumber, peeled and thinly sliced
1 tsp. sugar
1 tbsp. vinegar
2 tomatoes, chopped
½ small onion, skinned and chopped
½ green pepper or 2 small green
   chillies

¼ tsp. pepper
½ tsp. salt
2 5-oz. cartons natural yoghurt
Chopped parsley for garnish

Place the cucumber in a bowl, sprinkle with sugar and vinegar and marinade for 10 minutes. In another bowl mix lightly the tomatoes, onion, and green pepper; add the drained and seasoned cucumber. Mix with the yoghurt and garnish with parsley.

Saffron Rice

½ lb. Patna rice
2 tsps. salt
6 cloves
1 stick cinnamon
3 bay leaves

4 whole black peppercorns
½ tsp. saffron
2 tsps. milk
A little melted butter

Place all the ingredients except the saffron, milk, and butter in a pan with 1½ pints rapidly boiling water. When the rice is just tender, drain it, but do not remove the spices. Mix the saffron with the hot milk.

Place the rice in a dish and pour a little melted butter over it, followed by the saffron and milk mixture. Serve with meat curries. *Serves 4–6.*

Tomato and Apple Chutney

2 lb. apples
2 lb. tomatoes
¾ lb. onions
1 clove garlic
½ lb. dried fruit, seeded
¾ lb. sugar

½ oz. mustard seed
½ oz. curry powder
1 tsp. cayenne pepper
Salt to taste
1½ pints vinegar

Peel and core the apples and stew in a very little water until they are tender and pulpy. Cut up the tomatoes and chop the onions and garlic (also the dried fruit if necessary). Add these and the sugar to the prepared fruit. Tie the mustard seed in a piece of muslin and add it, with the remaining ingredients, including the vinegar, and cook gently for about 2 hours.

When the chutney reaches the required consistency, pour into hot sterilized jars and cover in the usual way.

Bombay Duck

A dried, salted fish often used as an ingredient in curries as well as an accompaniment. The smell when it is being prepared is rather unpleasant, but the taste is appetizing.

Bake in a hot oven or toast under the grill until crisp and brown; alternatively, fry in hot fat and drain well. Break the Bombay Duck into small pieces or crumble up and sprinkle over the curry at table.

Sambols

Coconut: Slice or grate fresh coconut and serve with chopped green and red peppers.

Desiccated coconut may be substituted for fresh, if necessary.

Peppers: Red and green peppers can be parboiled, sliced, egg-and-breadcrumbed, and then fried; or they can be sliced and used raw.

Bananas: Use firm bananas; slice and sprinkle with salt, lemon juice, and a little chilli powder.

Aubergine (Egg Plant): Boil until soft, then skin, mash the pulp, and add a little finely chopped onion, 1–2 chopped chillies, a little coconut milk to moisten, and salt to taste.

Cucumber: Fry a chopped onion and garlic clove in a little oil until soft but not coloured, add chopped cucumber, with a little crumbled Bombay duck and curry powder, a squeeze of lemon juice and a little coconut milk. Simmer until the cucumber is just soft. Serve hot or cold.

Tomato: Skin and slice several tomatoes, mix with some fresh or pickled green chillies cut lengthwise, a pinch of ground red chillies, and a squeeze of lemon juice; add salt to taste. Sprinkle with freshly grated or desiccated coconut and a little chopped onion.

Onions: Slice thinly and add lemon juice, seasonings, and some chopped fresh (or pickled) chillies.

Potatoes: Cut several cold cooked potatoes into cubes and blend lightly with a few chopped green chillies, a little finely chopped onion or spring onion, and some olive oil; season to taste and add a little lemon juice. Alternatively, mix some cold mashed potato with desiccated coconut, coconut milk, a little chopped onion, and a few coarsely chopped red chillies; add a little olive oil and lemon juice and season to taste.

Dried Peas: Soak the peas overnight, then simmer until tender, drain, and serve sprinkled with lemon juice and paprika pepper.

Eggs: Cut 2 hard-boiled eggs lengthwise into quarters and blend with 1 finely chopped small onion, 2 green chillies, coarsely chopped, 1 tsp. lemon juice, and salt to taste; sprinkle with fine desiccated coconut or fresh scraped coconut.

Pappadums: Thin wafer-like biscuits that can be bought in tins. To cook, fry one at a time in a little very hot fat until crisp, holding them down with a spoon as they swell in cooking. Alternatively, heat for 1–2 minutes under a hot grill.

CHAPTER 11
Desserts

Here are a few really different ideas for finishing off a meal. Again, as with the vegetables, they are particularly good to have up your sleeve if there's a glut at the height of the fruit season. And remember – many of these recipes can be used for other similar fruits, so why not experiment and widen your repertoire of desserts?

Danish Apple Cake

$2\frac{1}{4}$ lb. cooking apples
4 oz. sugar
4 oz. butter or margarine
4 oz. coarse breadcrumbs (preferably half white and half brown)

Jam or marmalade
Ground cinnamon
$\frac{1}{4}$ pint cream or top-of-the-milk

OVEN TEMPERATURE: 350°F (mark 4)

Wash, peel, and slice the apples, then stew them with or without a little water, according to type. Add half the sugar. Melt the fat and mix in the breadcrumbs, then add the remaining sugar, stirring this into the fat until light brown in colour. Grease an 8-in. cake tin and in it place alternate layers of crumbs, apples, jam or marmalade, and a light sprinkling of cinnamon, finishing with crumbs. Press down firmly, then cook for $\frac{1}{2}$ hour in the oven.

Turn it out and decorate the top with whipped cream and jam or marmalade; serve hot. *Serves 6.*

Apple Bake

$1\frac{1}{2}$ lb. cooking apples, peeled and sliced
6 oz. self-raising flour
$\frac{1}{2}$ level tsp. baking powder
Pinch of salt

$3\frac{1}{2}$ oz. butter or margarine
A 6-fl. oz. can of evaporated milk
4 oz. soft brown sugar
Cold milk

OVEN TEMPERATURE: 400°F (mark 6)

Sift the flour, baking powder, and salt into a mixing bowl. Rub in $1\frac{1}{2}$ oz. of the butter. In a small saucepan combine the evaporated milk, sugar, and remaining butter. Bring to the boil and bubble gently for 3 minutes. Meanwhile, mix the dry ingredients to a soft but manageable scone dough with cold milk. Roll out on a floured board, stamp into 2-in. rounds about $\frac{1}{2}$ in. thick. Place in a single layer in the base of a $3\frac{1}{2}$-pint shallow ovenproof buttered dish. Well drain the apples, arrange over scones, and pour the sauce evenly over the apples. Bake in the centre of the oven, uncovered, for 35–45 minutes.

Serve warm from the dish with custard, soured cream, or whipped cream. *Serves 6.*

Orange Liqueur Rice

1 orange
4 oz. short grain rice
1 pint milk
1 oz. sugar

2 oz. butter
1 oz. icing sugar
1 wineglass Cointreau or brandy

OVEN TEMPERATURE: 350°F (mark 4)

Using a potato peeler or sharp knife, peel the orange thinly. Shred this peel and place some of it in a buttered ovenproof basin with the rice, milk, sugar, and 1 oz. butter; cover with buttered paper and place the basin in a tin containing a little water. Bake in the centre of the oven for 2–3 hours, until the rice is cooked and the liquid absorbed.

Meanwhile, make the sauce by creaming 1 oz. butter with the icing sugar, adding the Cointreau or brandy, orange juice and remaining peel and beating gently. Turn the rice mould out and coat with the sauce. *Serves 5–6.*

Barbados Bananas

6 bananas, under- rather than over-ripe
4 oz. dark, soft brown sugar

4 tbsps. rum
Butter

OVEN TEMPERATURE: 400°F (mark 6)

Grease the pie dish thickly with butter. Slice the bananas lengthwise and layer in the dish with the sugar, finishing with a layer of sugar. Spoon over the rum and add some dots of butter. Bake for about 25 minutes. Serve warm with unsweetened whipped cream. *Serves 4.*

Baked Cidered Pears

4 firm eating pears, peeled
2 oz. Demerara sugar

A little mixed candied peel, chopped
1 pint cider

OVEN TEMPERATURE: 350°F (mark 4)

Halve and core the pears. Arrange in a layer in a shallow ovenproof dish and sprinkle with the sugar and candied peel. Pour in the cider and cover the dish. Put near the bottom of the oven and cook for about 1 hour.

Drain the pears and put in a serving dish. Boil the liquid until just thick enough to coat the fruit, then pour it over. Serve with cream. *Serves 4.*

Pears Brûlée with Orange Cream

2 large juicy oranges
Water
3 oz. caster sugar
8 firm ripe eating pears
4 level tbsps. soft brown sugar

1 level tsp. arrowroot
2 tsps. cold water
2 oz. butter
½ pint double cream

Thinly pare the rind from 1 orange, free of all white pith. Cut into very fine julienne strips. Squeeze out the juice from both oranges. Boil orange rind strips in water until soft; strain. In a large open pan, dissolve sugar in 1 pint water, bring to the boil, and reduce to simmer. Peel the pears, halve, and carefully remove the cores. Add the pears to the sugar syrup. Cover and simmer until tender – about 10 minutes. Drain.

Place drained pear halves, cut side down, in an ovenproof dish. Sprinkle with soft brown sugar and grill quickly until browning. Meanwhile add orange juice to the syrup and reduce by boiling to ½ pint. Reserve 3 tbsps. Blend arrowroot with 2 tsps. of water, add to the syrup, boil until clear, and stir in the butter. Pour over the pears, garnish with orange strips and serve slightly warm or cold with orange cream. *Serves 8.*

ORANGE CREAM
Place chilled cream and chilled, reserved orange syrup in a deep bowl. Whisk until the cream just holds its shape.

Pears in Port Wine (*left*) and
Cherries in Red Wine (*right*)

Pears in Port Wine

4 large pears
¼ pint port
¼ pint water
3 oz. sugar
Rind of 1 lemon
2 tbsps. redcurrant jelly (or to taste)

OVEN TEMPERATURE: 325°F (mark 3)

Peel the pears, cut in quarters lengthwise, and remove the cores. In a flameproof casserole, make a syrup from the port, water, sugar, and lemon rind. Add the pears and simmer gently until tender. Alternatively, cover tightly and cook near the bottom of the oven for 20–30 minutes. Remove the fruit, add the redcurrant jelly to the syrup, and boil rapidly until it is well reduced. Place 4 pear quarters in each glass and strain the syrup over. Allow to cool and serve with cream. *Serves 4.*

Peach Crispy-Top

1 medium-sized can of peach slices
 (approx. 10 oz.) or apricots or
 pineapple chunks
Grated rind of 1 lemon
1 oz. butter

4 oz. fresh white breadcrumbs
2 oz. desiccated coconut
2 oz. brown sugar
1 level tsp. ground cinnamon

OVEN TEMPERATURE: 375°F (mark 5)

Drain the fruit, place in an ovenproof dish (reserving some for decoration) and sprinkle with lemon rind. Melt the butter in a pan, add the breadcrumbs, coconut, sugar, and cinnamon, and mix well. Spread over the fruit and bake towards the top of the oven for 10–15 minutes, till the top is crisp and bubbling. Decorate with the remaining fruit. *Serves 4.*

An alternative topping is made by rubbing 2 oz. butter into 2 oz. brown sugar, 2 oz. plain flour, and 1 level tbsp. mixed spice, and adding 2 oz. chopped nuts; cover the fruit with this mixture and bake as above for 15–20 minutes.

Cherries in Red Wine

1 lb. red cherries
Red wine

2 tbsps. redcurrant jelly
Arrowroot

OVEN TEMPERATURE: 325°F (mark 3)

Put the cherries in just enough red wine to cover, add the redcurrant jelly, and stew gently, tightly covered, near the bottom of the oven for 20–30 minutes, until soft. Strain off the juice and thicken with arrowroot ($\frac{1}{2}$ oz. to 1 pint juice). Put the fruit in individual glasses and pour the juice over. Chill before serving. *Serves 4.*

Chocolate Pineapple Puddings

An 11-oz. can of pineapple pie filling
1$\frac{1}{2}$ oz. flaked almonds
3 oz. soft margarine
3 oz. caster sugar

3 oz. self-raising flour
1 oz. cocoa
2 eggs
1 tbsp. milk

OVEN TEMPERATURE: 350°F (mark 4)

Butter 4 $\frac{1}{2}$-pint individual ovenproof dishes and divide the pie filling between them. Scatter half the nuts over the pineapple pie filling. Place the remaining ingredients in a bowl and beat together until well mixed – about 2 minutes. Divide the mixture between the dishes. Spread evenly and cook for 25–30 minutes.

Serve in the dishes dusted with icing sugar, or turn out upside down onto individual plates. *Serves 4.*

If wished, a chocolate cake mix could replace the home-made sponge.

Chocolate Marshmallow Pudding

$\frac{3}{4}$ **pint milk**
1 egg
2 oz. sponge cake crumbs
3 oz. ground almonds

1 oz. cocoa
1 oz. sugar
1 tsp. vanilla essence
$\frac{1}{4}$ **lb. marshmallows**

OVEN TEMPERATURE: 350°F (mark 4)

Heat the milk and pour it on to the well-beaten egg. Put the dry ingredients into a bowl and pour on the egg and milk, add the sugar and vanilla essence, then pour into a greased dish and bake until set – about 1 hour. Remove from the oven, arrange the marshmallows on top and brown them under a hot grill. Serve with marshmallow sauce – see recipe below. *Serves 4.*

MARSHMALLOW SAUCE
4 oz. granulated sugar
3 tbsps. water
8 marshmallows

1 egg white
Vanilla essence
A little colouring

Dissolve the sugar in the water, then boil together for about 15 minutes. Add the marshmallows, cut into small pieces with scissors. Beat the egg white very stiffly then gradually fold in the marshmallow mixture. Add essence and colouring.

Index